LUCID DREAMING

LUCID DREAMING

USE YOUR PSYCHIC POWERS TO EXPLORE
THE WORLD OF YOUR DREAMS

Tony Crisp

A GODSFIELD BOOK
www.godsfieldpress.com

To Akela
For travelling with me
and to
All of you who dare to explore
beyond the frontier

First published in Great Britain in 2006
by Godsfield Press,
a division of Octopus Publishing Group Ltd
2–4 Heron Quays,
London E14 4JP

Copyright © Octopus Publishing Group 2006
Text copyright © Tony Crisp 2006

Distributed in the United States and Canada by
Sterling Publishing Co., Inc.
387 Park Avenue South, New York, NY 10016-8810

A CIP catalogue record for this book is available from the British Library.
ISBN-13: 978-1-84181-290-8
ISBN-10: 1-84181-290-0
10 9 8 7 6 5 4 3 2 1
Printed and bound in China

Contents

What is lucid dreaming?

Sleep is a strange country. In it you lose your sense of self, or your dreams take you into realms of extraordinary experience in which you are still largely unaware. But throughout history there have been individuals who have described a different meeting with sleep. They wake up in what is usually a dark, unconscious world. Or, in the midst of a dream, they become aware of the situation and relate to their dream in a new and dynamic way.

This condition, usually called 'lucid dreaming', holds within it enormous possibilities that are generally unavailable in waking time, sleep or dreaming. To understand these possibilities and also something of what takes place during lucidity, it is helpful to appreciate that during sleep your five senses are largely switched off, and while you are dreaming your voluntary muscles are paralyzed.

Usually you enter this sightless, soundless, immobilized world of sleep without awareness. However, travelling consciously beyond sensory input into the substrata of your mind and body is an incredible experience: you then enter sleep with all your critical faculties, with active curiosity and with the ability to explore whatever you find. When you become lucid in sleep you carry the bright torch of personal awareness into the depths of your body and mind.

CROSSING THE FRONTIER

This is a frontier that only a few people have crossed. Like the frontiers of sea and sky that past generations overcame, the frontier of awareness holds enormous treasures and benefits. However, unlike the frontiers presented by exploration of the oceans and space, this one is open to all. To wake fully in your sleep and dreams is one of the most amazing adventures you can have. Climbing a mountain or travelling to wild places is exciting and interesting, but discovering your roots and exploring the depths of your mind and your heart are

life-changing. Even the techniques leading to lucidity bring life-transforming change into your everyday life.

In becoming lucid, you not only enter the world of sleep – with all of its possibilities of extended memory, creativity and healing – but discover a world of experience that is beyond the limitations of waking life. Imagine what it is like to reach for creative ideas and find them; to create a world around you that brings peace; to be able to practise new skills or improve old ones with expert tuition; or to follow your curiosity in almost any direction, with full access to whatever you have read or learned in the past. And you are able to *live* these things, and not just think them. You can explore love and relationships with wonderful sensitivity, and even step beyond the usual barriers of time and space – experiencing yourself in a variety of roles or in different periods of time.

In lucidity, not only do you begin to tap the enormous potential within you, but you also release something of that potential into your waking life. Lucid dreaming is not a Disneyland of ephemeral entertainments; it is the doorway to real personal growth and adventure.

Voyages in lucidity

My first experience of lucidity occurred when I was 15 and had been practising a method of relaxation. One night I fell asleep while using the technique. Instead of losing awareness, I continued the descent into sleep with full consciousness. This was an incredible experience, because I could feel my body senses being turned off. Thinking disappeared and instead I was aware of a profound ocean of peace. For the first time ever I knew that life offered much more than I experienced while awake, and I had the sense of existing without need of my body.

Usually someone's earliest experiences of lucidity are less dramatic. The following example, related by William, is fairly typical of early experiences:

My family and I got out of our car. As we talked, I realized there was a motorbike where my car had been. I said to everyone, 'There was a car here a moment ago, now it's a motorbike. Do you know what that means? It means we are dreaming.'

So I asked them if they realized they were dreaming. They got very vague and didn't reply. I asked them again and felt very clearly awake.

Although such flying experiences are interesting, they do not illustrate the creative, learning and personal growth potential of lucid dreaming. Wildlife ecologist Bruce, in reporting his own explorations of lucidity, explains one of its creative possibilities, writing:

For many people their early experiences of lucidity are linked to flying. Jill describes one such dream as follows:

There is a crowd watching me, to whom I explain that I can fly, since this is a dream. I soar high in the sky, touch clouds and return to Earth. I experiment with several variations in styles of flying. For example, I fly backwards while standing, and direct my flight by choosing the distance of my visual focus.

In a few lucid dreams I play the piano, and play it like a concert pianist. My 'real' keyboard skills are all by ear, self-taught and at best rudimentary. But in the lucid dream state I've had fun with this ability and spontaneously composed some wonderful classical pieces, as in a concerto. At times I awoke with the musical composition still fresh in my mind. The pieces were complex, beautiful, moving and, as far as I can tell, thoroughly original and spontaneous. These dreams have shown me that we probably all have a tremendous capability for innate creativity and composition.

Note that Bruce does not simply daydream about being able to compose spontaneously – he actually does so. This is one of the wonders of lucid dreaming: you experience things in a full-surround virtual reality that activates all your senses and abilities. Usually, however, you do not leap into such full-blown creative lucidity. Like most other things, lucid dreaming is a learning process. To arrive at your creative power you may need to deal with the feelings or fears that prevent you being at your best in waking life. Unfortunately, some dreamers avoid this, as Alan describes:

> *In many of my dreams I become aware that I am dreaming. Also, if anything unpleasant threatens me in the dream, I get away from it by waking myself.*

TRANSFORMING EXPERIENCES IN THE WORLD OF DREAMS

Bearing in mind that suppressed grief and strained emotions are connected with a higher incidence of physical and mental illness, this is not a healthy way of dealing with your fears and emotions. However, there are ways of transforming them. The following examples illustrate an unusual type of lucidity, and potential ways to deal with a life problem. Francis explains:

> *In my dream I was watching a fern grow. It was small, but opened very rapidly. As I watched, I became aware that the fern was an image representing a process occurring within myself, one that I grew increasingly aware of as I watched. Then I was fully awake in my dream and realized that my dream (perhaps any dream) was an expression in images of actual events occurring unconsciously in myself. I felt enormous excitement, as if I were witnessing something of great importance.*

Breaking through the imagery in this way to the processes and possibilities underlying your dreams is a royal road to discovering your own innate talents. You can transform negative memories and habits, and use your creativity to deal with real-life events. Jon describes just such a transforming experience:

I am in a landscape and notice that everything is brown; the whole world is brown and lifeless. There is also a feeling of solemnity or dullness. I have enough lucidity to wonder why the world of my dream is so brown and dull. As I ask this, I become more aware of what feeling the brownness expresses. It is seriousness — with no room for humour or fun. The feeling deepens, being real enough and clear enough to look at and understand. I see it is my father's attitude to life that I have unconsciously inherited. I realize how anxious he always felt about life, and how I took this in. That is how I became a 'brown' person. I see too that

I do not need to be either brown or serious any more. Then the landscape changes. There are trees, plants and animals in brilliant colour. I wonder what this means, and the landscape begins to spin until the colours blend and shimmer. Suddenly my body seems to open to them, as if they are spinning inside me, and with a most glorious feeling, a sensation of vibrating energy pours up my trunk to my head. With this comes realization. I see how stupid I have been in my brown, anxious existence — how much life I have held back. The animals and plants are the different forces in my being that blend into energy and awareness. I feel I am capable of doing almost anything, like loving, writing a song, painting, telepathy or speaking with the dead. This sparkling, vibrating energy is life itself and can — if I learn to work with it — grow into any ability or direction that I choose. I wake with a wonderful sense of my own possibilities.

A new world to explore

For a few moments, think of yourself not as a body with five senses, but as a point of awareness. Now visualize yourself being mobile. You can, as in dreams, be a bird flying, a cloud floating, in deep-sea diving gear, or any other sort of equipment or form.

While you are awake, your point of awareness is locked firmly in a particular type of equipment: your body. Usually you think of your body as yourself. But for a moment I want you to see it simply as something like a diving suit that you have put on. While awake, you are clothed in this 'suit' all the time, so it is like a glove that you forget you are wearing. But, in going to sleep, you take that glove off. While sleeping, your senses switch themselves off. You lose all sense of your body shape and size. While dreaming, your voluntary muscles are paralyzed. You have stepped out of your personal diving suit.

Over millions of years the human body has evolved to deal with particular situations – survival in the physical environment of the planet's surface. This equipment only has limited senses to deal with the needs of immediate survival, with some space for improvement. But life itself – the magical and mysterious process that formed you – can be almost anything. Look around you at the creatures existing in sea, air and earth. In sleep you return to being unclothed, in a state prior to the forming of any body, any suit. You return to the root of life's immense possibilities. You are naked awareness. In your dreams you can therefore be anything at all.

FINDING YOUR ROOTS

Think for a while of what that means. At the moment of your conception you started a journey from the earliest forms of physical life on this planet. You moved through various stages of growth (almost like being a plant, then a fish, then an animal and then taking on mammalian form). But even at birth there were further journeys. You started absorbing the culture into which you were born, and the language and beliefs of that culture. Your naked awareness took on level after level of 'clothing'. Becoming aware, as an individual person, was yet another layer that you put on.

Perhaps you identify totally with the person you have become. But if you had been born into another culture, you would now have different beliefs and a different response to the world. Who then are you, at your roots?

Fundamentally you are a million possibilities – as is life itself. In sleep you touch that wonder of yourself, beyond all the clothing you have taken on. You touch your unbounded potential, even though (as in dreams) you struggle to make it conform to the waking person you are convinced you are. Becoming lucid in sleep enables you to start the exploration of what you want to become; the building of the life you want to create for yourself; the channelling of that extraordinary potential into your waking life.

Benefits and possibilities

It has been recognized that you can benefit from the experience of dreaming and lucid dreaming in the following ways.

PROMOTE PHYSICAL AND PSYCHOLOGICAL HEALING

In the second century CE three hundred healing temples that used the power of dreams still existed throughout Greece and the Roman Empire. There are records of both physical and psychological healing being achieved there. In our own times, the imagery and drama of dreams are regarded as something like a book cover – interesting, but merely as an illustration of the massive information held beneath the cover. By asking the question as to what lies beneath the surface of a dream, enormous insights can be gained and healing changes achieved. Lucid dreaming has the potential to speed up that transformation, because you enter the very heart of the dream process with a searching question.

The imagery in your dreams is a way of communicating with usually unconscious

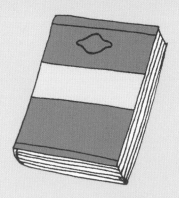

body processes. Once you grasp that, you can begin to work towards self-healing. Lucidity enables you to enter into yourself and reprogramme your 'wiring', offering you an amazing means of self-help.

SOLVE PROBLEMS IN YOUR DAILY LIFE

Everyone has enormous problem-solving abilities. When you learned to talk, there was no college professor or dictionary to help you. You learned the meaning of hundreds of words without ever having looked in a book. Similarly you have absorbed an unbelievable amount of information simply by living and – out of the corner of your eye, as it were – taking in millions of bits of information about life. You absorbed most of this without really being aware what you were taking in. But at times you acknowledge it as a 'gut feeling' or intuition. This comes from things you learned in the rough and tumble of life, not in the schoolroom.

Dreams and lucidity take you beyond the surface level to where all those stored lessons of life exist. There you can draw on an immense hoard of information and experience in order to solve problems. Your conscious problem-solving ability deals only with things you have already organized into words, or have formulated into clear ideas. But a large amount of your experience still remains disorganized; it does not readily jump into words or clear ideas. It has to be gathered together by a question and a particular state of mind. Dreaming is that state of mind in which the ocean of experience can be explored, and where it expresses itself as drama and imagery. Lucidity is the creative act that transforms imagery into insight and creative problem-solving.

PRACTISE LIFE SKILLS

A researcher at the University of Pennsylvania found that cats with damage to a particular part of their brains would live out their dreams in movement. These cats would stalk, crouch and spring at imaginary prey. He concluded from this that one of the functions of dreaming is to practise life skills.

Lucidity enhances this possibility. Dreams are a world in which there is no risk of any hurt. You can explore relationships, life situations, new skills, your own creativity or sexuality in this world of limitless possibilities. When lucid, you can choose to meet any person to learn from or relate to. You can place yourself in any situation, ready to explore. All you face are your own emotions, experiences and thoughts. The world that you weave with these is up to you, for in dreams *you* are the creator.

FIND YOUR TRUE POTENTIAL

So-called 'unintelligent' small birds have learned to fly from one end of the world to the other without a compass. Life – alive in them, and in you – has drawn that skill out of its limitless possibilities. As a human being, you have the self-awareness to ask questions and seek out what you are capable of. You can tap into whatever it is that enables birds to travel the world. As Jon said earlier (see page 11): 'This sparkling, vibrating energy is life itself and can – if I learn to work with it – grow into any ability or direction that I choose.'

We often believe that people who are creative or who achieve great things are somehow different or more gifted than we are. Or we excuse ourselves by saying that their life circumstances gave them a better start. Maybe they did have a more advantageous start in life, but that doesn't mean you lack potential or creativity. Remember that every night your dream maker creates a uniquely different drama. That fount of creativity is alive in you. If you are not using it, because you don't believe in yourself – well, step into the temple of your dreams and get a good helping of belief. Drink from the source!

DISCOVER YOUR DEEP HISTORY

Lucidly entering your dreams can give you something few people ever find: an experience of connection, of continuum and of memory beyond your years. You are connected to everything around you – just as your finger is connected to your hand, and your ear to your head. They have an independent existence, but in no way are they disconnected; they could not exist without your body. Neither do you exist without the universe. It has an influence on you that is as intimate as your body's connection with your finger.

Similarly, you do not exist independently of your forebears. In the same way that the tree of today carries an aspect of all previous trees from which it sprang, so you carry within you an immense history. It is both the history of life and the history of your family. The deeper you dig into your dreams using lucidity, the more of your own history you will uncover. With lucidity you can discover your odyssey through time, space and eternity, you can enter the realm of your ancestors and appreciate what an extraordinary being you are.

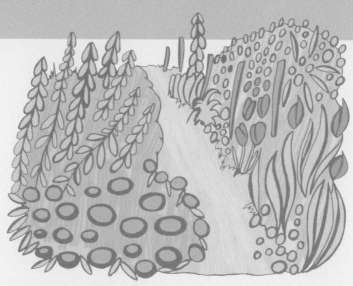

UNFOLD YOUR EMOTIONAL AND SEXUAL SELF

Your growth is like that of a plant. As a tiny seed you were fertilized and began to grow. There were stages to your growth and different possibilities (not all of which you may have achieved). The acorn holds the potential of a mighty oak, but the tree may not achieve its full potential. Similarly you may not have managed to blossom in life, or may not have produced all that you are capable of. Perhaps some of your emotional, mental and creative energy is frozen or did not have the opportunity to develop. The process of growth that developed you from a tiny seed holds the potential of further growth. If you work with awareness in the garden of your dreams, that blossoming can take place. There is more love, sexual satisfaction and self-worth for you to unfold.

EXPLORE THE UNIVERSE WITHIN YOU

The psychiatrist and dream explorer Carl Jung described the unconscious as something we must not ignore. He said that it is as natural, as limitless and as powerful as the stars.

Dr Stanislav Grof, head of psychiatric research at the Maryland Psychiatric Research Center and an assistant professor of psychiatry at Johns Hopkins University School of Medicine, spent many years collecting evidence from people who were exploring their unconscious. At first he could not believe his findings. However, proof continued to grow that people could remember their experience as a baby in the womb; and they could recall verifiable information regarding their forebears and describe past cultures in detailed ways (including the form and meaning of various amulets used in Egyptian mummification). In fact, people were able to transcend all the accepted boundaries of what is possible. Dr Grof concluded his findings by saying that he had no doubt that the present view of the universe and the world around us – what we call 'reality', and especially our understanding of what it is to be human – is superficial, incorrect and incomplete.

Unfortunately many people carry a belief of their own limitations. There is also doubt as to whether what is experienced is real or merely imaginary. The simple solution is to test what is experienced, to see if it works in your waking life. There is a whole universe to discover within you. Go and explore it!

EXPERIENCE ECSTASY

Underneath all your everyday concerns, worries and unrest lies a state of blissful peace. You are like the ocean: on the surface a storm may be raging, but at the sea bed all is calm. To bathe in this bliss beneath the surface is deeply healing and nourishing. It does not take away your worldly motivations or concerns, but it

does bring renewal and strength in dealing with them. Fiona describes this as follows:

I felt a slow dawning of something soft and beautiful in me. It emerged from a deep silence within and filled me with a feeling of radiance, as if my being was gently shining. I literally felt and saw a shining light from within. I knew this radiance would alter the way I relate to others and would also penetrate them. I felt I could love easily and without grasping, and it didn't matter what happened in a relationship.

Dreams as a doorway

In 1978 Dr Bernard Siegel, assistant clinical professor of surgery at Yale University School of Medicine, started 'Exceptional Cancer Patients', which was an individual and group therapy using patients' dreams, drawings and images. Recognizing that dreams gave patients an insight into what their body was doing, Dr Siegel started a campaign to make more people aware of their own healing potential. Many other doctors have expressed similar findings – namely, that dreams can reveal the deep workings of the body and may be used to promote the self-healing process. A psychiatrist at the Leningrad Neurosurgical Institute, Dr Vasily Kasatkin, came to this conclusion following a 41-year-long study of 10,240 dreams collected from 1,200 patients.

My own experience leads me to liken dreams to the monitors we see at the bedside of hospital patients. On the monitor there is a visual representation of what is happening unconsciously within the patient. His pulse, blood pressure, respiration and even his brain patterns can be shown visually on the monitor. However, in dreams (especially lucid dreams) the images and drama are – like computer desktop icons – linked to the inner functions they portray. Click on the icon and it stimulates a response. Two-way communication can take place, and the dream image is directly linked to what it conveys. So when you are lucid you can literally work with sick parts of your body and help them to heal. Or you can seek out answers to specific questions about the health of your body and mind.

YOUR WONDERFUL BODY–MIND

One researcher into body–mind therapy calls such dreams 'X-rays of the Unconscious'. But of course they are much more than that. Elizabeth, now 50 years old and living in Vancouver, dreamed at the age of 24 that she was looking into a treasure chest with a skull and crossbones on it. When she opened the chest, it was full of bread. On waking she knew that the dream was warning her not to eat bread. She went on to discover that she was suffering from coeliac disease (an intolerance of the gluten found in most breads) and that bread was harming her. So her dream was not simply showing her an illness in her body, but was suggesting what she could do about it, by saying that bread would harm her.

In his book *Love, Medicine and Miracles* (Rider, 1999), Dr Siegel gives examples of such directly informative dreams. Although scientific research has not yet been able to establish the how and why of these dreams, the countless thousands of them experienced by ordinary women and men show that there is something in the depths of your being that responds to your needs and enquiries.

Sometimes such dreams come spontaneously, but they can also happen because you have asked for help or insight. This is why it is important not to simply wipe away dreams that disturb you or that you don't like. They are messengers, and you need to work *with* them and transform them through understanding. Jon's experience of his brown landscape (see page 11) is an example of this. He didn't reject the brownness; he explored it and it transformed itself, because he realized that he didn't need to be 'brown' any longer.

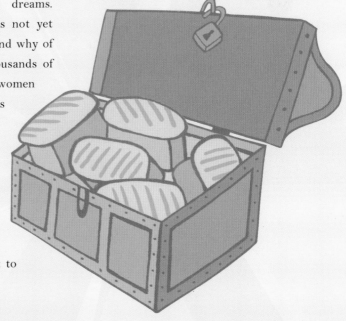

Entering your dream world

Most people know the saying 'Use it or lose it'. They know that the mind and body require exercise and stimulation to maintain their present quality and develop further skills.

The innate ability that you have to move beyond the boundaries of your everyday world of experience also needs to be exercised and stimulated. A story of a grandfather who was apparently on his deathbed illustrates this. The old man loved playing the fiddle and had spent many wonderful hours teaching his grandson how to play the instrument. Now, alone and with such joy ebbing from him, he seemed to be sinking fast. But then his young grandson arrived, sat with his grandpa, quietly took out his fiddle and played something. His grandfather's eyes

opened, and the miracle of renewed love and pleasure soon had the old man sitting on the edge of his bed and joining in the shared music.

Your body and mind are the most amazing instruments, and there is so much more music for you to play as you move to a fuller life. An early step in learning how is to begin remembering and recording your dreams. In so doing you will be taking the first steps into lucidity. In fact, recalling a dream means penetrating the unconscious with your awareness.

Your dream maker is in some ways as shy as a deer in the woods, and in other ways as ready to please you as a dog that loves you. This part of you is certainly as old and as natural as the creatures of the forests. Like any creature, it is moved by feelings, by curiosity and love. Therefore your first step in recalling your dreams lies in stimulating interest in that usually hidden world within you. Remember that a lot of great art arises from the unconscious in dreams and from unbidden inspiration. Sigmund Freud wrote, 'Not I, but the poet discovered the unconscious.'

So open yourself once again to those things that you find moving and beautiful or that arouse passions in you, and allow your curiosity to question what other wonders are still unknown in you.

REMEMBER YOUR DREAMS

Use the steps in this exercise to help you recall your dreams and become lucid. First, you need to find an object, a picture or a piece of music that stirs a sense of the best in you and in life. People use things as varied as a symbol of their religious belief, a picture of a family member they love, or something from nature that depicts for them the wonders of life.

1 Before going to sleep, take a few minutes to dwell on your chosen object. While doing so, hold the thought that the wonder or love you feel is the beginning of a stream of influence that arises from within you. This sense of beauty can also communicate with you through your dreams, so ask it to help you remember them. Your intention in recalling your dreams is important: it directs your attention to the subtle dream process that can so easily be ignored or lost in the welter of waking impressions. Keep your intention playful, as you might with a good friend. Don't let early failures bring negative feelings.

2 If possible, avoid taking sedatives or stimulants — such as coffee, alcohol, tea, cocoa derivatives or a heavy meal — before going to sleep.

3 Put a notepad or small tape recorder near your bed so that you can record any dreams you remember. Dreams melt like snowflakes on your hand unless you record them quickly. This is especially so of dreams recalled during the night. A tape recorder is probably easiest, because you do not have to put a light on or rouse yourself too much in order to use it.

4 As you start to fall asleep, wonder what strange world of beauty or learning your dreams are going to explore. You normally dream about five times a night, so you will certainly have a different life in your sleep. Wonder what that is, and determine to ask yourself what you have dreamed as you start to wake during the night or in the morning. What is life telling you in your dreams? Build an image of yourself remembering a dream and recording it.

5 When you wake, don't move or open your eyes. This floods your awareness with massive new impressions and can blast the dream memory away. Tests also show that the passage of time (even just a few minutes) between dreaming and attempting to remember causes many dreams to fragment and be lost. So lie still for a while and look backwards into the dimness of sleep. Imagine yourself drifting back to the place from which you are just emerging. Leave your mind like a keyboard that can be played by subtle feelings and images. Having given time for your dream to emerge, record it right away.

6 Write your recalled dreams into a dream journal: either a good thick book or a computer file (the latter has the advantage of being easy to search through later on, so it is worthwhile noting any themes, characters or places that appear). A dream journal is a precious resource and will gradually develop into a record of your most intimate and whole self. It can become a rich mine of inspiration, creativity and insight into yourself and your waking endeavours.

7 When you have written up your dream, think about it as a drama that reflects your own hidden nature. Ask yourself what the images depict. This is not an attempt to interpret the dream, but a necessary technique to make you aware that dreams are merely like a book cover: what is important is what lies underneath.

8 A number of other exercises are given throughout this book. However, it is advisable not to hurry on to these until you feel you have succeeded in the goal of the particular exercise with which you are currently working.

First steps in becoming lucid

Becoming lucid in your dreams is all about extending focused awareness into areas of yourself in which you are usually 'asleep'. This is why the first stage of lucidity is remembering your dreams; in doing so, you extend your perceptions beyond your everyday waking experience.

Carl Jung taught that your waking personality is only a small fraction of who you are. He described it as a small, bright spot on the surface of a large sphere. The sphere as a whole he called the Self.

The Self includes all the conscious and unconscious parts of you. Extending focused awareness means taking the brightness of waking awareness into the unexplored aspects of your wholeness. Becoming lucid means extending that awareness even in everyday life.

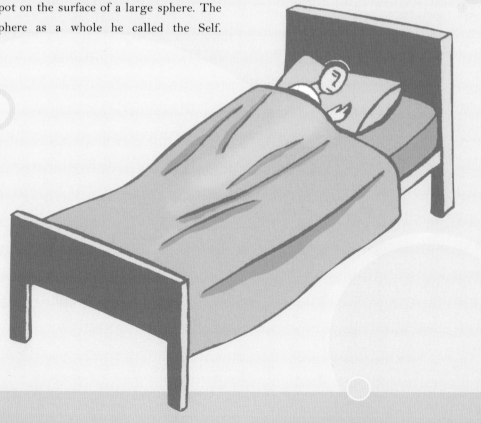

WAKE UP TO NOW

This exercise should be done for at least a week before moving on to the next exercise. It involves taking in a more total experience of where you are and what you are doing, and performing this several times each day.

1 You may be barely aware of your body for most of the day. Or you may be so focused on what you are thinking, working on or worried about that you are unaware of subtle feelings or what is going on around you. So take a few moments to notice what is happening in your body. Are you tense or relaxed? What is your posture expressing?

2 Move from that to noticing what you are feeling. On a scale of ten, is your mood low or high? Notice what is on your mind.

3 Now, staying generally aware of your body and mind, take in your surroundings. Listen to the sounds and feel the atmosphere. Notice how you relate to the people around you and to the world in general. This can be done in any situation, even in the midst of talking or doing something else. Aim to do this at least four times each day. As you do it, ask yourself if you are awake or dreaming, or are you lost in the whirl of events and impressions?

4 You should do this exercise until it becomes habitual. Then it will transfer into your dreams and lead you to ask the same question: Am I awake or is this a dream? If you are dreaming and you become lucid, the question then becomes: Am I lost in the whirl of events and impressions of this dream?

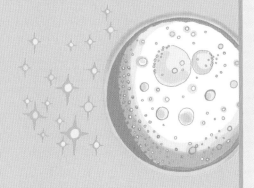

THE DREAM HOME

This exercise catalyzes an even more penetrating type of awareness that will begin developing your ability to gain insight into your life and dreams. This is fundamental to real lucidity, so do not hurry through it.

1   Sit somewhere comfortable in your home: take time to find somewhere that you most like and where you feel most relaxed. Using the focused awareness described in the previous exercise, sit and look around you, but not in a critical way. If possible, view your surroundings as if they are new to you and notice what impressions you get. See if you can sense the atmosphere of the place. Do not read on until you have achieved something of this.

2   Now look around you as if you are in a vivid dream. Remember that a dream is a full-surround virtual reality. All of its features are reflections of who you are and what you feel. This is proved conclusively by lucid dreamers being able to be any of the characters or objects in their dream and even transform them. Similarly you have

transformed your surroundings to some extent. Even if you are in a hotel room, you have probably put personal possessions around you and have changed it from how it looked when you entered. So what is your home saying about you? What of you is it reflecting? The following description that Simon gives of returning home when he was in a condition of lucid awareness gives a graphic example of this:

When I walked through the garden gate I noticed things about the garden I had never let myself see before; the untidiness and absence of care were no longer hidden by veils. The track I had worn across the small front lawn particularly caught my attention. It was there because I used it as a shortcut instead of walking round the path. But then I arrived at the door and knew suddenly that it was all me. The door was me, and every scratch on its paint was a part of my life, reflecting who I was. Opening the door, I went into myself. The door and garden had

already shocked me with my lack of attention to outer details. Now, inside the house, the same things showed themselves in the state of my home, depicting my inner health. But I also saw the beauty of my children, and how, despite my self-absorption, I had helped make a warm home for them.

3 Don't fret if your response is not as pronounced as the one quoted above. It is enough just to look around and let your feelings and thoughts respond spontaneously. This is not an exercise in concentrated thinking or analysis; it is an opening to spontaneous or intuitive responses and a way of penetrating your usual way of seeing things or responding to your surroundings. The shift is brought about by looking at the outside world as a reflection of yourself. Your home surroundings are particularly useful because they most reflect your qualities. But they must be looked at as if in a dream, with the question: What do my surroundings depict of myself? This question, if used frequently, will become a catalyst, promoting new perceptions.

4 Use the exercise frequently and, as you gain results from looking at your home, turn your attention also to your relationships, to work or to any other aspect of your life, such as your clothes.

Taking control of accelerator, brake and steering wheel

If you purchased a machine that was as complex and as wonderful as yourself, you would demand a handbook from the manufacturer. Unfortunately, the universe, the planet and the parents who brought you forth do not supply such a helpful guide. Yet there are things about the way you work that it is incredibly useful to learn about.

In some ways you can be likened to a car. You have an accelerator, a brake and a steering wheel. Most of the time these are applied unconsciously by external controls. Running, making love, drinking coffee or watching a powerful film will cause your body and mind to become more excited; your breathing and heart rate will speed up – this is like pressing the accelerator. Drowsing in an armchair or drinking alcohol represents the opposite

and slows you down – this is the brake. As for the steering wheel, other people or events influence you and your direction.

However, you can learn to press your own accelerator, apply your own brake and take more control of the steering wheel. Knowing how to use your own controls, instead of having them constantly activated by other people or events, is a life-changing skill.

LEARNING TO DIRECT YOUR BREATHING

For a start, if you recognize that breathing reflects excitation or quietness, learning to direct your breathing is one way of taking control. So try slowing your breathing down for a few minutes. Do not hold your breath; simply make your breathing as slow and smooth as you can, without having to gasp for air. It helps if you sit or

lie quietly. You can count as you breathe, to help regulate the cycle. Being aware of the slow passage of air at your nostrils aids the sense of calmness. Find a rhythm that is slow, but not making you breathless, and over time start to lengthen the cycle.

This gradually changes deeply seated habits of a lifetime. Taking hold of the breath and controlling it is like taking hold of your nervous system (or body) and gradually altering the way it responds to events and thoughts. It is like gently taming a wild animal. There should be no force or conflict involved. Practising this for ten minutes each day for three months will change the way you respond to triggers that cause stressful responses.

Being at the driving wheel of your own life means that you are not swept away by emotions and urges, such as anger and sex, unless you want to be. Equally it means that you can let yourself be spontaneous, if you wish. It means you can direct your feelings, mind and body wherever you choose, without avoiding places where fears or urges deny you access. In the realm of dreams this is vital – otherwise a scary dream can send you scurrying away from something that holds vital personal information, or from releasing frozen energy and potential that could add enormously to your effectiveness and physical health. It also develops the strength you will need to become lucid.

Shifting gears by learning to relax

I once witnessed a noisy argument (almost a fight) between two men on a London bus. One man was an agnostic and the other believed firmly in God. Being so rigidly stuck in a belief has led thousands of men, women and children into terrible wars over the years. Most people have such constraints, sometimes to the point of

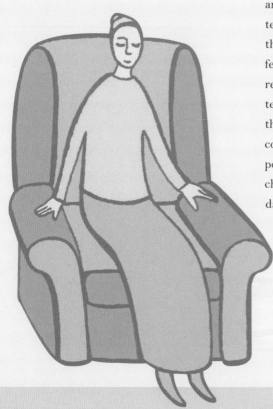

paralysis. In the world of dreams they can literally create an inability to make use of your potential – you can't run, talk and defend yourself in your dreams.

SHIFT BETWEEN TENSION AND RELAXATION

You can shift between being tense and relaxed. Take time each day, while sitting, to close your eyes and slightly tense your anus and face. When you are aware of the tension, slowly relax. Gradually repeat this, tensing less and less, until you can feel the difference between the tension and relaxation – even if it is only a feeling of tension and a feeling of relaxation. Allow the sensation of letting go of tension to continue, even as you move from a sitting position. Take your time learning this, and check your tension levels frequently each day until it becomes an effortless habit.

LEARN TO LET GO

You can move from active to passive, and back again. Adult life can be partly summarized as the effort to maintain control. This means you attempt to control your body movements, emotions, speech and where you are going in life. As important as this is, letting go of control is also necessary, but is a lesson that few people learn well. If you cannot let go of control, you cannot go to sleep at night, for sleep is the ultimate letting go. Also, many important processes within you cannot surface if you control what you experience all the time. Your body–mind heals itself by doing things you might not consciously like, such as vomiting poisonous food, producing scary dreams and discharging stressful emotions in an attempt to heal old traumas. If your control went too deep, you would die very quickly.

That is why most of the vital life processes are beyond your control. To get into the realm of the most vital parts of your mind and body, you need to learn a little bit of humility – of letting go.

WATCH WHAT YOU EXPERIENCE

Learning to relax is the first stage in letting go, but it is still a form of control. When you are in a relaxed state, develop an image or sense of your vital life process – what it is that makes you breathe and your heart beat. Now imagine you are opening to the process that moves your heart, makes you breathe, and you are ready for it to move you in any way it wishes – to move your thoughts, emotions and body. Take on a passive observing and allowing attitude, and watch what you experience. You are like a keyboard ready to be played.

Crossing the threshold

The previous exercises and techniques have been a graded, step-by-step approach to gradually learning a different way of bringing you to a deeper connection with your life process. Whatever you do when you become lucid, you are basically experiencing a closer relationship with this process – with the usually unconscious functions of life that cause you to exist. Of course, the same holds true in a normal dream. But in lucid dreaming you begin to cross an amazing and evolutionary threshold, on the way to becoming a new type of human being. You are developing a fresh self-awareness; you are learning to extend that relationship with life and enter new possibilities and a new world.

All memories are unconscious until you call on them. You use the doorway of memory all the time, so you already have an open doorway to work with. Your breathing is another such connection with your unconscious self, and in slowing your breathing you are widening that doorway. You are now going to build on what you have already developed.

You should not attempt the next step until you feel you have a good working experience of the previous exercises. There is no danger in this step into the unconscious, but it might not work until you have learned to slow your mind and body by directing your breathing, achieved a relaxed state and found some degree of letting go. The unconscious cannot express its more subtle side unless you have learned to let go of conscious control in some measure.

WHAT DID YOU DREAM?

This exercise offers you a technique to let you enter more fully into your memory. It is also a test to see if you can cross the frontier of sleep while awake. You will then become lucid directly from the waking state, and will recover something of which you have never previously been aware. You can do this at any time of the day, but you need quietness and at least ten minutes when you will not be disturbed. If there is no other opportune time, you could do it just before going to sleep or just after waking up.

1   Close your eyes and ask yourself the question: What has been dreamed? You are not looking for already remembered dreams, but for one you have never previously recalled. Because you have no idea of the subject or image of the dream, you need to leave yourself wide open to all possibilities. Think of standing in a stream of images and ideas, and letting them all drift past you without interference until the right one comes.

2   When the actual memory comes, you will have an immediate realization that this was a dream, despite all the other images. When you succeed with this, you will know that you have truly delved deeply into yourself – into lucidity. And this is a great thrill.

Memory techniques: waking attitudes and sleep cues

When you consciously cross the frontier of sleep, you will learn that there are two levels of will or decision-making in you. Both are familiar. The first is conscious decision-making. The other you often forget about: it is the will that keeps you alive. If you hold your breath, and keep holding it, you will feel the strength of that will pushing against that decision.

This will is an expression of the universal life acting within you. That same will circulates your blood and attempts to keep you healthy, despite the many things you

might do in acting against it. It expresses itself in sleep as dreams and spontaneous movements or speech. It is enormously important and powerful, and you have started a fuller relationship with it in the breathing and relaxation exercises.

Some years ago I taught dreamwork at Atsitsa on the Greek island of Skyros. Windsurfing was one of the activities there, and I watched raw beginners struggle to keep their balance and repeatedly fall into the warm waters of Atsitsa bay. But, by getting back on the boards and trying again, the surfers effected a transformation within a few days. The waves were the same, the boards were the same, but now the surfers were in balance and harmony with the forces of wind and waves around them, and they flew over the sea. This is exactly the relationship you are seeking with the powerful forces that you will meet as you cross the frontier of sleep – not control, but learning to ride and move with the energies within you, towards the goals you wish to reach.

A waking attitude is being defined here that you will carry into your lucid experiences, enabling you to 'surf' that ocean more skilfully. The attitude is one of watchful awareness in the midst of letting go. Being too much in control keeps you in the shallows of the lucid experience – it is like trying to stop the waves or the tide. It is far better to work with their energy and learn how to use them to your own advantage.

CARVING IN SPACE

This exercise helps you to develop that vital waking attitude.

1 Stand with your feet slightly apart in a space in which you can easily move your arms and body.

2 Relax and close your eyes, and extend your arms sideways as far as they can go, without tensing them.

3 Now start slowly circling your arms across the front of your body. Focus your awareness on your fingertips, noticing the shapes you are making in space. Continue this for a while, being aware of the shapes you are carving.

4 When you have a sense of this, be aware of what sort of shapes your hands and arms want to carve in space, if you simply let them move wherever they want to. Give yourself 15 minutes of this, allowing your body and even your voice to enter into the spontaneity if they want to.

5 Go with whatever feelings arise. Hold the attitude that what you are doing doesn't have to make sense. Nor does it have to comply with what other people might expect of you. Realize that you are allowing another part of yourself – perhaps a non-verbal part, or a facet unknown to the rational mind – to express itself.

6 Write up what you experience in your dream journal (see page 25).

What arises from this exercise will often be expressed as symbolic movements or mime. You are thus entering directly into the world of sleep and dreams while you are still awake. It is important to recognize that symbols are an attempt on the part of your deeper nature to communicate with you. So think about the significance of whatever is met. Gradually you'll find this open, watching, questioning attitude will lead to direct insights while the process is going on. What you learn while awake will then enter into your sleep and bring lucidity.

The above exercise needs to be done until you get easy results. As with all the exercises in this book, don't move on to the next exercise until you are well versed in the current one. So far, the exercises have led you to step gradually over the frontier of sleep. You have begun to develop a relationship with the world that is active on the other side of that frontier. The next step is to consciously go further into that territory of your inner self by developing a deeper relationship with it. Here are two exercises to help you cultivate this.

REALITY CHECK

Many things that you do during the day you are also bound to do while you dream. Common examples are walking through a door or meeting someone. The 'reality check' is a way of linking the waking act with the dreaming one.

1 Use one or both of these examples (meeting someone, for instance), and each time you meet someone, ask yourself whether you are awake or asleep. If you make a habit of doing this, it will happen when you dream and will lead to lucidity.

2 Just before you go to sleep, imagine yourself using the reality check in a dream, and becoming lucid. Say to yourself, 'I am going to do the reality check every time I meet someone in my dreams, and I will then become lucid without waking.'

THE SLOW BREATH

For thousands of years meditation has been seen as a doorway to the wider awareness of lucidity. In fact, some masters of meditation say they are continuously lucid throughout sleep. Their lucidity does not arrive through clever techniques; just by gradually widening their everyday awareness beyond the norm.

1 You have already been using one of the most powerful meditations: directing the breath (see page 31). Now you should prolong your practice of the slow breath, so that its influence can deepen and gradually transform you. Use the practice of slow breath every day for at least 20 minutes. It will repay all that you put into it, in many more ways than with lucidity.

2 This is not an easy meditation, because it takes discipline, but practise it until you find that your breathing is slower when you are at rest. You can then move on, although you will find yourself returning to this meditation in many of the exercises that follow.

What to do when you become lucid

It is important to make a habit of seeing your surroundings and your dreams as depicting yourself in some way. Read again what Jon said about the transformation that arose from recognizing what his dream 'brownness' indicated (see page 11). Grasp as firmly as possible how a dream is an expression of your own mental and emotional self. This helps to stimulate lucidity and aids you to prolong it once you achieve it.

If you find lucidity slipping away, it is helpful to use the slow breathing meditation (see page 39), which assists you in calming and riding the situation. Some people find that if they imagine themselves spinning like a top, this also keeps them from losing lucidity.

When you first become lucid it will be a tremendously exciting experience, and may happen in a flying dream. The excitement arises because you know from deep within that you have achieved an amazing breakthrough. The sense of freedom is enormous. But if you have no idea of what is possible, you may stay lucid, but simply roam around in the dream imagery. So take some time to imagine what you might like to do, with the following possibilities.

NO BOUNDARIES

Explore the freedom open to you beyond the dangers and limitations of your body. You can fly, swim underwater without breathing, jump from a high building without danger, make love in any way you like, take on any shape or any gender you wish, experience being an animal or a tree, or living in any period of time. In other words, you can play and revel in this world, safe beyond any danger. Playing with the virtual-reality world of dreams requires you to learn how to direct and move the imagery around you. This comes from

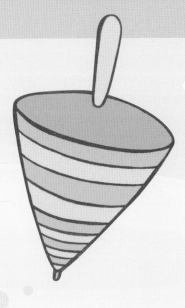

practice. It all arises from changing your feelings and your thoughts, and using your imagination. Whatever you imagine can become real in lucidity.

FINDING ANSWERS

Find useful or practical answers to almost any question. This does not require the sort of laborious thinking that you use in study and exams. It is a matter of taking on the 'keyboard' condition described earlier (see page 25), and holding the question in your mind. The answer comes intuitively, but you must let the answer create what you see and experience around you. Someone might appear and talk to you and give you an answer.

Search out the roots of personal problems, fears or failings. This is done in the same way as seeking answers to a question. It takes more courage and discipline, though, as you may need to meet strong emotions and memories.

FIND WHAT DRIVES YOU

Clarify your destiny. Do this by exploring the main drives and passions in your life, and where they come from. These drives are like great underground rivers that flow into many of your motivations and actions.

How to use the experiences you may have

No matter where you live, if you look around you, your surroundings are either largely or wholly shaped by human action. Your home was at one time merely an idea in someone's mind. Materials were then moulded to make that idea a physical reality. Humans constantly shape or reshape the world around them, both individually and collectively.

In lucid dreaming this becomes accelerated to an incredible degree. Shift your mood in a dream and your whole surroundings change. So the overall situation you are going to meet is that you are the creator of the images, characters and experiences that you encounter. Of course, at first the creation is going on unconsciously. Your hopes, past traumas, ideas and creative impulses, your underlying potential, are shaping what you experience in your dream. This is why the gear-shifting exercises were given (see

pages 32–33). And slow-breath meditation (see page 39) is vital in meeting the world you inhabit in your dreams. So use the imagery of remembered dreams to practise shifting your feeling and mental states, and utilize this in dealing with your lucid experiences. Do this by imaginatively reshaping the dream towards a more fulfilling conclusion.

Something that lies behind the creation of many of your dream scenes is the process in you that attempts to keep your body and mind healthy. This will manifest as recurring themes or situations that confront you again and again. Honour that process by learning to work with it. What it requires is the ability to observe and question constructively. For instance, if the theme of a lost or hurt child appears often, then you would need to ask the question: 'What situation in my life does this reflect?'

DEVELOPING WIDE-BEAM AWARENESS

Findings regarding the difference between right-brain and left-brain operation show that most people live in a narrow, focused perception most of the time. In lucidity there is a wide-beam global awareness. This wider vision is an extraordinary enhancement of your normal way of learning or experiencing. You will encounter this 'wider awareness' again and again in lucidity. Test it and assess what you gather from it, just as you would test any other source of information. Often it is like a wise teacher, in that it gradually unfolds deeper and deeper understanding in you about certain aspects of your life.

The teachings of the major faiths around the world say there is something of great value to find at the core of human life. Many explorers of lucidity say they have found this pearl of incomparable value. It is the direct experience of their very essence, and is beyond life and death. They touch something that lies beyond time and space, that is beyond change. In different cultures it has different names. Nevertheless, it lies within each of us and does not have to be earned. It simply exists. Finding it may radically transform your values, altering the direction of your life. So open yourself to its influence, as from it arises your potential.

GOING DEEPER

Deepening your skills

FINDING YOUR TIMELESS SELF

For instance, the cells in your body are unbroken subdivisions of cells going back to the beginning of life on this planet. In that sense, your body is millions of years old and carries the sum of that experience. What would it be like for your awareness to expand to include that timespan? What would it be like to remember not just your dreams, but your infancy, your life in the womb or your life in eternity? Lucidity is not simply playing within dream images. It can also be remembering who you are in your entirety, and what part you play in the scheme of things. Your present personality (even with great schooling) is just a young thing developed during the life of this body. But it is riding an ancient and wonderful life-form, and can find unity with that.

Tracy, who has long explored lucidity, describes her experience of this as follows:

Suddenly, towards the end of exploring my dream, I leaped beyond anything I had ever experienced before. I knew, just as clearly as in ordinary life I know my name, that instead of being someone separated from everybody else, living a certain day in time, my real self was a river that flowed through all time. I had always existed and was involved in all history. With an amazing heightened

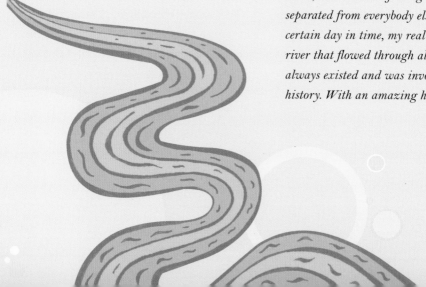

awareness I could see the influence from this timeless self flowing through all my present life, subtly shaping it. The things I had chosen to do, or work at, were all connected, as a working out of ancient influences or an attempt to change them.

For the next few days, take some time to imaginatively trace your body backwards. Remember that the cells of your being can never generate from something dead. So move backwards through all your conceptions, all that collected history in your genes, all that change and time. See if you can get a feeling of that vastness. Ask yourself what is it in your being that has survived through all the vastness of time, and are you in touch with it? It is wonderful to have that glimpse into the mind during lucidity. But lucidity is not something that happens only during sleep. Perhaps the most inclusive description of lucidity is that it is expanded awareness. To understand this you have to move beyond a view of the world based on the limitations of your physical senses.

Incubating lucid dreams

During the period of writing this book, while walking home along a main country road (one I had walked many times), I suddenly felt a fear of the cars passing me. It was strong enough to make me walk as far away from the road as the pavement permitted. As I walked on, wondering why I felt such fear, a van pulled up beside me on the road to take a turning away from me. As it stood there waiting for the traffic to clear, and as I was passing it, I heard the scream of tyres as a car went into a skid on the wet road. Then the skidding vehicle shot up onto the pavement between me and the van. It was an extraordinary intuitive experience.

I have had many such things happen to me, because I have tried to listen to that wider awareness in which our 'little self' lives. What happened to me walking along that road was one form of lucidity – and the more lucid you become in your dreams, the more this wider awareness will become a feature of your life.

If you have made a habit of doing reality checks, you have probably experienced lucid dreams by now. But there are ways in which your lucidity can be made even more frequent. Don't forget, though, that remembering your dreams is the most powerful method of increasing lucidity. Meanwhile, here are some ways to bring about more lucid dreams.

CREATE A HELPER

You can create an external helper by making a tape recording that plays while you are asleep. The tape is intended to work with the reality check (see page 38).

1 Get a long-playing tape (a 120-minute cassette), or if you know how to burn a recording onto a CD, use that instead. You can put quiet background music on most of the tape if you wish. This will keep you nearer the surface of sleep, enabling more frequent lucidity.

2 The important point is to have the words 'You will now do a reality check' spoken about an hour into the tape. This should then be repeated just before the tape ends. Put the same recording on the other side, so that when the tape ends you can simply turn it over and let it play again (or repeat the CD tracks).

3 This is like having a friend sitting with you through the night, gently reminding you to do a reality check as you sleep and dream. By turning the tape over (or setting the CD to replay), you can have the prompt reminding you throughout the night. Obviously the volume needs to be fairly low, so as not to wake you completely.

4 As you go to sleep, say to yourself over and over, 'When the tape reminds me to do a reality check, I will become lucid in my dream.'

OTHER TAPED MESSAGES

The tape method is extremely powerful and, allied with continued reality checking, needs to be continued until you become lucid often enough to start exploring and discovering the possible wonders of the lucid experience. As that happens, take time to use some of the suggestions in this book concerning what you can do while lucid (see pages 40–41). This is like learning any other skill and needs practice, so do be patient.

As the taped message begins to work, you can introduce many other messages played in the exactly same way. If you seek an answer to a problem, you could record the following words on the tape: 'You will now do a reality check while dreaming, and while lucid will seek an answer to...' (then add what it is that you want to find out). In this way you could use the external helper to explore any areas of lucidity, such as finding your innate direction in life, satisfying love, and so on.

GROW YOUR OWN SEED

Here is a waking exercise that you can do when you have the time and inclination. It helps to develop the 'keyboard' condition (see page 77) that is so important when trying to access some of the possibilities available in lucidity.

1 Create a space (about a single blanket in size) in which you can move without banging into things. You need to be in a place where you will not be distracted or disturbed for up to 30 minutes.

2 Wear loose clothing and, if you wish, play some music that does not grab your body with its beat.

3 Stand with your eyes closed and your feet slightly apart. Raise your hands above your head towards the ceiling (or sky, if you are outdoors).

4 Hold in your mind the idea or image of a dried seed. You do not need to concentrate. Simply let your body take on the keyboard condition and watch to see if your posture expresses what shape you feel a dried seed would be. Follow that feeling until you find a position that you sense is right.

5 Once you are reasonably satisfied with your position, imagine what a dried seed might feel like inside. Is it waiting, sleeping, unconscious? Whatever you imagine it to be, let your own inner condition be as nearly like that as you can make it.

6 Then let your seed be planted in warm, moist soil. Just as you followed the keyboard condition to find the 'seed' position, follow it in the same way to see how your body and emotions will express the growing

seed. Don't worry if you have no urge to move, and only wish to stay in the warm. Many people find that this meditation has its own dynamic and that they can only grow to a certain stage, or that the unfolding story throws up unplanned details. These details of how your own growth occurs in the meditation are relevant to your life situation. Just follow whatever arises for you.

7 Note in your journal what you experience, and try the exercise again within about five days.

Prompts to wake you in your dreams

The methods you have used so far to help you become lucid are powerful enough, but if you need an extra boost to take you into lucidity, the following techniques should do it for you.

After you have used this method for some time, try the next exercise. One or the other approach should suit your particular temperament. In fact, as you enter more fully into lucidity, you will find

THE WAKING DREAM

For this exercise you need to remember a dream that is clear and vivid.

1   As soon as you wake, with the dream still in your mind, use the relaxation techniques (see pages 32–33) to release any tension. Then imagine yourself entering into the dream, just as if it were a real environment. Feel the atmosphere, look around you, sensing what you did in the dream. Take your time with this and, as you look around, notice what is dreamlike or different from your waking awareness. Learn to recognize what these signs of dreaming are. It might be that things change rapidly, or you are intimate with people you don't know. Go over the recognition of these signs of dreaming until they are easily remembered. Use this with each dream that you recall. And, as you do so, say to yourself mentally that in future dreams you will recognize these signs and become lucid. In fact, imagine what it would have been like to become lucid in this dream through recognition of the dream signs. Allow yourself to change the dream, or to experience it in any way you choose.

2   Repeat the process again, telling yourself that in future dreams you will become lucid. Explore your dream, noticing what is dreamlike about it. Instruct yourself that in future dreams,

very personal tuition arising from your dream experiences which will suit your circumstances and personality. Until then, however, use these methods to deepen your experiences of lucidity.

when you meet these signs, you will wake in your dream and begin to access its treasure. Visualize waking up in your dream and experiencing the things you want to gain from lucidity. Keep repeating the process for at least ten minutes before you finish.

3   If you miss out on this process as you wake, you can do it during the day.

4   While you dream, your brain produces all the signals to your body that, if you were awake, would promote physical movement, speech and emotions. However, a small area of the brain blocks these signals so that you do not move around too much while you sleep. Even so, the movements and sounds you make in your dream are important and form part of your memory of it. Therefore, if you have the time and space to do so, imagine yourself walking into the dream and actually make some of the movements, sounds and postures in your dream. This acts to restimulate the deep levels of memory. When you have done this, act out what you would do and feel in becoming lucid in your dream.

EXTERNAL REMINDER PROMPT

This approach is based on a method suggested by Bradley Thompson in his excellent two-CD *Lucid Dreaming Kit*. It is perhaps the most powerful method and, if it is used after you have done the previous exercises, will certainly take you into greater lucidity.

1 Purchase a digital wristwatch that gives an audible beep on the hour. Set the watch to sound every hour. Wear it during the day, and every time you hear the beep, look at the watch and do a reality check (see page 38). You must do this until it becomes a habit, for it is the habitual response that is the important factor. Building the habit takes the action and reality check right into your unconscious, where it will act with hardly any awareness – as in sleep.

2 Do this for three days. Then place the watch near you as you sleep, so that you can easily hear the hourly signal. As you go to sleep, repeat over and over again for a minute or two, 'When I hear the hourly signal, I will do a reality check in my dream and become lucid.'

3 Use this method for as long as you wish. The more you use it, the more effective it will become.

4 As with the other techniques, when you attain lucidity, start giving yourself goals to achieve. To start with, it is enough just to play in the lucid experience, to discover the unbelievable freedom that you have and the completely safe environment you are in. You can swim underwater without breathing; you can fly, either as yourself or as a bird; you can become any of the characters in your dreams, or any character in history or the present. These are play things, and you can later move on to matters that are of greater importance.

THE LUCIDITY SCRIPT

Here is a script that you can put onto tape to encourage lucidity.

1 Read the script slowly so that it plays that way. Say the following words aloud into the tape recorder:

Imagine standing by an immense and beautiful ocean. Create a feeling or an image of this ocean. This is not an ocean of water, but an ocean of life and consciousness. This ocean pervades all space, enters into all things, and is the source of your own awareness. You emerged from it at birth and began the journey of this life with a sense of separateness. But now you are ready and strong enough to accept your part in that ocean and to open more fully to what it can offer you. Ask for help from it on your journey of further growth – of widening awareness. As you request this, you are allowing the protective layers of yourself to melt sufficiently for you to become more aware of this ocean of life from which you emerged.

2 Play the tape to yourself as you practise your relaxation or slow breathing. Think of the words used only as a suggestion, not as an attempt to state any absolute truth. They are a means to enable you to open up to your own wonderful potential.

Are there dangers in spreading your wings?

There are dangers in virtually everything we do in our everyday lives. People die from normal activities, such as driving a car, eating out and the electricity in their homes. We take it for granted that knowing and avoiding such dangers is a regular and normal part of life. So it is good to look at the possible dangers of crossing the frontier into wider awareness and exploring lucidity.

FAILING TO UNDERSTAND LUCIDITY

Years ago Steven was trying to develop his intuition. He was going to use a crystal ball to do this, and was convinced that pictures and scenes actually appeared in the ball, rather than the ball acting as a focus for his mental imagery. That lack of understanding could have put Steven in a dangerous relationship with his own imagination and imagery, for he would not arrive at a balanced evaluation of what he was experiencing or feeling.

The danger of such a lack of understanding applies to lucidity, too. You are dealing with powerful mental, emotional and spiritual processes, and it is important to understand what the dream process is capable of and what it does. Remember: a dream is a full-surround virtual reality activating all your senses and abilities. When you are in it, it is just as real to you as the physical world. But there is a huge difference. The environment, people, animals and objects are all projections. In the film *Matrix* the hero is at one point put into a lucid virtual reality called 'the construct'. He cannot understand what is happening to him, and his guide says, 'What you see now is what we call residual self-image. It is a mental projection...' Your dream is exactly that: an amazing moving and living projection, in which you act and interact with *yourself.* There is nothing else, in the widest or cosmic sense. The process of dreaming transforms your emotions, your beliefs and hopes, your fears and traumas, your intuitions and creative visions, into people, environments, animals and events. Understanding that is vital.

AVOIDANCE OF YOURSELF

The second danger is avoidance. Because everything you meet is an aspect of yourself – either your small or cosmic self – any avoidance of a frightening dream figure or difficult environment is an avoidance of yourself. The figures and environments are created out of your own mental, emotional and sexual energy. Avoiding them means losing portions of your own potential and your own physical and emotional energy. I know this as a vital personal truth, because at one time I suffered from what is now called ME (myalgic encephalomyelitis, or chronic fatigue syndrome) and was so tired that I barely wanted to stand up. However, as I reclaimed my dream figures, the tiredness disappeared.

Your dream characters and animals are intelligent and purposeful. They have a semi-independent life within you until you integrate them. You create them unconsciously, using your energy, positive feelings and motivations. Avoiding them leads to loss of your full potential and health. I am not suggesting that you should immediately meet and integrate all your many aspects. That takes time, courage and a form of strength that grows only as you mature in this new environment. What is important is to remember your goals: integration and wholeness, growth into a new level of ability and maturity, a new connection with others and with yourself. You do this by claiming and loving all that you are.

FAILING TO UNDERSTAND
YOUR OWN ABILITIES

In crossing the frontier into your fuller life, you have opened a gate wider than you have in the past. Usually only a few dreams and feelings have been allowed through into waking life, and for some people not even dreams have emerged. So it is important to remember that the world of lucidity can sometimes emerge into waking life, if it is important enough. Sometimes there is an urge from within that needs to be known and breaks through in the form of a waking dream. That sounds easy, but remember that a dream creates a full-surround virtual reality. When the breakthrough occurs, you may see people, hear a voice talking to you, or see an animal that is not physically present. If you do not understand the process, you may become anxious about it. So take this in and make it something you understand. A vision, a hallucination, is the dream process occurring while you are awake. It is not a sign of madness, but an indication that you are now able to access your intuition and unconscious senses more capably.

NOT KNOWING YOUR TERRITORY

The fourth danger – not knowing your territory – is not a major threat, but it can be disturbing if you are suddenly in an environment of which you have no understanding or concept. So recognize that there are five major levels of awareness, each of which produces very different ways of experiencing yourself.

Level 1: waking consciousness

The attributes of this level are focused awareness through the physical senses; a limited perception of, and ability to change your surroundings; the ability to reason deductively and inductively; critical observation.

Level 2: dreaming

Without lucidity, dreaming loses the ability to reason and critically evaluate situations. In it you are immersed in a world of your own creation that is infinitely variable and easily open to change. You unconsciously create an apparent reality expressed as dream images and drama.

Level 3: beyond the images of dreams

At this level you directly observe the forces of mind and body that create the dream imagery. Usually to enter this level you need to be lucid, otherwise it expresses itself as dream imagery. Here you can work directly with the body–mind processes.

Level 4: dreamless sleep

This level is usually experienced as unconsciousness. If entered lucidly, it becomes an infinite ocean of awareness in which you are an integral part of the cosmos and all that exists therein. Here there is the possibility of gaining insight into the way your present personality was formed out of this ocean of possibilities and collective experience.

Level 5: totality

In some cultures this level is called enlightenment or liberation. In this phase you are both the ocean of consciousness and individual waking awareness at the same moment.

What out-of-body and near-death experiences reveal

Out-of-body experiences are a powerful form of lucidity. Rachel describes her own vivid experience below:

When I was eighteen and living in Germany, I was woken from sleep one summer evening by a sensation of rushing upwards in darkness and a release from pressure. When I could see, I was looking down on my sleeping body and experienced terror, because something was happening to me that I had no explanation for. Then suddenly I realized I had read that some people experience leaving their sleeping body. That is what was happening to me. I had left my body behind and was still conscious and independent of it. The terror disappeared and I found myself curled up with my arms around my knees, flying over the countryside, which was still light because of the summer evening. But suddenly I was in my home in London, standing behind our couch. I felt more awake than I had ever been before in my life. I was amazed at what was happening. I seemed as solid as ever, despite having no physical body. My mother was sitting knitting, alone except for our Alsatian dog asleep in front of the gas fire. I was so excited that I called to my mother, 'Look what's happening, Mum. She paused for a moment, but carried on knitting. This puzzled me, as I seemed completely solid and real to myself and couldn't understand why she couldn't see me. So I shouted to attract her attention. She carried on knitting, but as I shouted the dog heard me, awoke and came bounding over to me, barking and howling to see me. I later found out that my mother had been alone that evening, and the dog had suddenly rushed to the back of the settee, barking and howling.

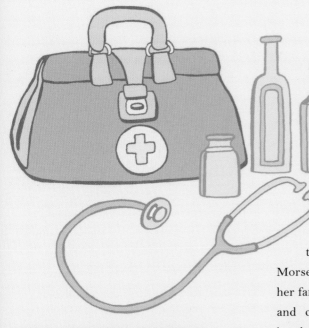

KATIE'S NEAR-DEATH EXPERIENCE

Dr Melvyn Morse specializes in the care of young children. Katie, a young girl, had been found floating face-down in a swimming pool and was brought to Dr Morse, apparently dead. A scan revealed that her brain was abnormally swollen. If not dead, she was certainly in a deep coma and was placed on a ventilator that breathed for her.

In his book *Closer to the Light* (Ivy Books, 1991) Dr Morse describes how Katie made a full recovery. He had to find out how she came to be face-down in a swimming pool, so he interviewed her and, to his amazement, Katie described the operating theatre in which she had been placed while she was in coma. She also described the other medical staff who were working on her and what they were doing. And she told Dr Morse that she knew what was going on in her family home while this was happening, and could describe in detail what her brothers and sisters were doing. In fact, it seemed as if she existed in a different state of time and space.

Dr Morse went on to investigate hundreds of such cases in a long-term study, and followed up on the children's stories, recording their experiences of out-of-body awareness during their apparent death. Of course, many authorities try to explain such experiences away, if they have not undergone them themselves. Dr Morse examined the possibility of drugs or other substances influencing the brain, and found that these did not apply. Again and again

people witnessed and reported actual happenings around them while apparently unconscious or without a heartbeat. His long-term study revealed that none of the children who had a near-death experience (NDE) exhibited any signs of drug use. They rebelled little against authority, and showed a keenness to learn and be active in the world. Their maturity and wisdom were marked, and each claimed that during their NDE they had learned profound lessons about the meaning of their life.

BEYOND THE LIMITATIONS OF SPACE AND TIME

Because we often believe that what we see in the physical world is an ultimate truth, we have the concept that distance takes time to cover, and that our body is the very foundation of who and what we are. Many people do not believe there is anything to learn from within them. They hold the view that there is only one reality – and that is the physical world and all it offers. They believe this despite the fact that consciousness is an extraordinary miracle, and imagination is a profound argument against everything occurring in the exterior world. Such ideas have given rise to mistaken views of the world that we enter in lucidity. As can be seen from Katie's experience, when she was released from the domination of her five physical senses, she had a completely different relationship with time, space and the people around her.

This points to an astounding possibility: beyond the limitations of the world that you know through your five senses, your mind or core consciousness can move around and live in a world not limited by time and space or the needs of your body. In this world within you lie enormous resources of information that are deeply relevant to who you are. From it you can gather insights that clarify the most important lessons

you face in this life, as well as your greatest talents and best direction.

Some aspects of modern physics suggest that, at a fundamental level, the separate parts of the universe are totally and immediately connected beyond distance or time. If you add awareness to this, it is stating that consciousness fills the entire universe beyond the limitations of space and time. It also suggests there are possibilities open to you beyond your imagination – if you reach out for them! Near-death experiences, out-of-body experiences and lucidity give you an intriguing insight into that amazing world of timeless, spaceless personal awareness.

I am not asking you to take that in and believe it all at once. Just hold it lightly, like a beautiful flower, and perhaps you will discover it for yourself as you explore lucidity.

Will you be a traveller
of wider possibilities?

Memory is a good example of how the unconscious and conscious work together; how the known and unknown meet and pass backwards and forwards. It also helps you to understand how an enormous breakthrough can occur. For instance, a huge mass of your experience and potential lie unknown in you. To illustrate this point, I am going to ask you a question – the answer to which is at present unconscious to you. When I ask the question, try to notice (if you can) how the answer becomes known to you.

The question is: What is your present home address?

As you see, something that was not on your mind suddenly appears. It's quite magical how this occurs!

You could be asked questions for hours or days, and still discover more information within you. You might uncover parts of yourself that had never before been known to you. However, what you are moving towards in lucidity is something beyond that. Supposing you are trying to remember somebody's name and are searching your memory under the letter B, whereas in fact the name is Jane, and you should have held in mind the letter J in order to trigger the memory. Holding the B in mind could act as a block.

FINDING THE RIGHT TRIGGER

Certain things in you need the right trigger. This is a basic truth in nature, where plant growth and animal mating are activated by the duration of light, temperature or other triggers. While most of your personality unfolded through infancy, childhood, youth, adolescence and maturity, and occurred spontaneously, there is another level of growth open to you as a human being that needs to be triggered to emerge.

As with adolescence, it isn't a case of developing this through personal effort. It is more like riding the wave as the development takes place – except that it will not usually occur until the trigger calls it into action. And, like adolescence, it is the birth of a completely different way of experiencing the world. Something new and splendid is born in you. Examples of the birth of this new level of growth are seen throughout history in outstanding men and women. But we live in special times, and many more of us are ripe for this new and wider life. As a species, humans have gone through enormous, and almost inexplicable, changes. From being mammals that had no self-awareness or complex language, humans made the huge jump to self-awareness, with its explosion of cultural and eventually technological development. But, as a species, we are ready for the next big change – linking the personal with the whole.

Natural processes (largely unaided by you) have carried you, like a current, through enormous physical and psychological changes to your present situation. Not only did you develop personal awareness – something unique in the natural world – but also personal will, to some extent. What the next step involves is a linking of your personal will and awareness with the natural forces that brought you this far. In fact that is the trigger: the opening of your personal will and awareness to the core life processes that cause your existence.

Opening the gates of mind and looking beyond

In 1969 I was lucky enough to spend time with the psychiatrist R. D. Laing exploring the unconscious. At the time I had an unforgettable experience of lucidity, which, after all these years, remains a fount of inspiration and guidance. I had relaxed deeply and entered a state of lucidity in which I felt as if I was falling down a very deep hole. This wasn't frightening, but reminded me of Alice in the rabbit hole. As

I fell, I passed through memories of things that had hurt me during my life – like the time I broke my nose. Then I hit the bottom, experiencing a womblike feeling of great peace. I realized, as I observed, that it wasn't the womb, but the very basic level of my personal awareness. But there was still a current carrying me back further, and I resisted, fearing that I would lose my identity. Then I suddenly understood there

was nothing to fear. I did this every time I went to sleep – trusting myself to the bosom of the deep. So I slipped into what I call the 'ocean of consciousness', and it caught me and started growing me, as if from a tiny seed. As this happened I knew that it was this power that had developed me in the first place, and that there was so much more of me to discover than I presently knew. Then the immense Life spoke to me. 'Come to me each day like this (in surrender) and I will grow you.'

Western science has in the past painted a picture suggesting that nature and the universe are one vast, impersonal and almost mechanical process. When you travel beyond the frontier of your own personality and contact the life that gives you existence, a completely different viewpoint emerges. What you find is the mysterious love that leads a crocodile mother to carry her babies unharmed in her mouth; the wonder that drives birds to fly hundreds or thousands of miles to an exact location to mate again with their dedicated partner; the indescribable beauty that lies behind a flower's miracle of colour and intricacy. You meet the creative impulse of the universe that has woven your being throughout eternity.

YOUR PART IN THE SCHEME OF THINGS

Within the meeting between yourself and Life lie all the other possibilities: the healing of your ills; the finding of a meaningful place in society and the world; the solving of problems; the discovery of creativity; peace. If any of that seems

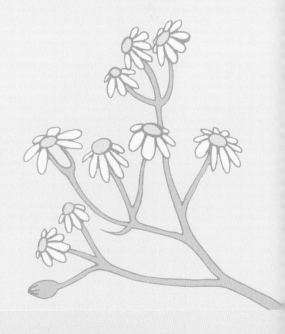

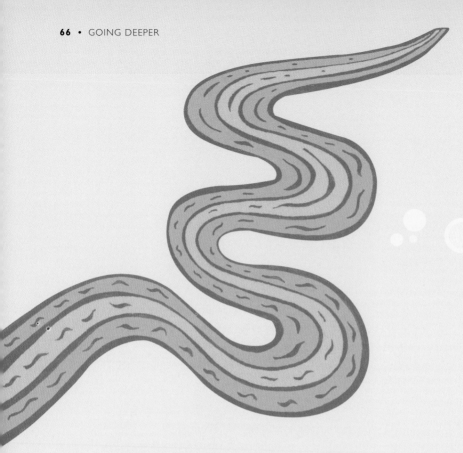

abstract, take a few moments to look at yourself. If you feel you are not totally connected with the processes of nature and of this planet, consider these points:

- You are a river. Water flows through you all the time. Without water, you would not exist.
- You are the wind. Air flows through you all the time. Without air, you would not and could not exist.
- You are the earth. The body of the earth flows through you in the form of food. Without substance, you could not exist.

You are totally and inextricably a part of the wind and the rivers and the earth.

Lucidity is a growing awareness of that. Lucidity is a greater consciousness of the part you play in the scheme of things, and the personal attitudes, pains and conflicts that stand in the way.

All of the previous exercises and techniques have been ways of gradually looking beyond the limitations of your physical senses and exploring the frontiers of a new level of awareness. There is no reason why you should not continue in that way and be an explorer. At this point, you can choose to take the first steps in becoming a new being. You can choose to open up to the process of life at your core and become a co-worker with Life.

OPEN TO YOUR CORE

If you wish to open yourself to that new influx of growth, take the following steps:

1 Take time to clarify what you feel lies at the core of your existence. You are not being asked if you believe in God. No such belief is necessary. If there is a God, you will find it at your core without any belief – just as you know the wind on your face without having to believe in it. What you are being asked is whether you brought about your own existence, and if you completely know who and what you are. If you do know, then you need read no further. If you are uncertain and believe that you are probably a mass of chemical, biological or energetic responses, ask yourself again if you know deep down that you have the final answer. If you admit that you do not know for certain, you can take the next step.

2 The state of not knowing is important. It frees you of preconceived or rigid ideas and opinions that might stand in your way – so this step requires no belief. What it does require is a sense that there is something you do not understand that brings you into being. Take time to develop this condition of not knowing.

3 When you feel the open condition active within you, state in some way that is an expression of this pivotal moment in your life, that you want the unknown mystery at your core to emerge more fully into your experience. A possible statement is: 'I come with all my being held open to the action of the mystery that is my core self.'

4 Considering that in the environment of dreams, and therefore of lucidity, you experience a world that you create out of your own beliefs, ideas and attitudes, it is fundamental that, until you learn to become empty, all you will experience is what you already hold to be true and believe, or are frightened of. Learning the condition of openness or 'unknowing' allows for the emergence of a new level of your own growth. Use it each day.

Developing a relationship with Wonder

In Chinese teachings about widening awareness, there is a series of ten woodcuts called *The Ox Herding Pictures*. The second woodcut illustrates the hero/heroine discovering the footprints of an ox in the mud. It depicts the realization that there is another power active in your life, other than your conscious thinking and will. In the pictures the hero/heroine goes in search of what has caused the footprints.

By now you too will have felt, in your dreams and in the exercises, the signs of another level of intelligence and purposefulness, other than that originating from your conscious personality. A new type of relationship is forming in you. It is a relationship with your core self.

It is no exaggeration to say that, as this relationship grows, you will realize that you are walking hand in hand with Wonder. You will at times know that you are standing close to a beauty you never knew before. You will begin to understand that you had somehow been blind since childhood, and are now being healed of your blindness; you were in some ways paralyzed, and are now learning to walk. Yet the relationship is not always an easy one. It starts a cleansing process during which old fears and hurts rise to the surface, to be washed away. Wonder asks something of you – just as love does in human relationships. And in some measure Wonder asks you to give yourself. But you are not left empty (as in some cases of human love).

EXPERIENCING YOUR CORE SELF

The author Raynor Johnson calls it 'The Imprisoned Splendour' in his book of the same name (Pilgrim Books, 1989), and that's what it is. Your act of searching for it and opening to it, releases it from its imprisonment within you. But remember that it may have been bound and gagged for so long that when you first unbind it, it may only be able to mumble incoherently and may barely be able to move. Be patient.

Nurture it; come to it often, and let it trickle or pour into you.

The writer J. B. Priestley, after his own meeting with Wonder, described it as a sort of white flame, trembling and dancing. He went on to say that he had never before experienced such happiness as he did then. Wonder never takes any definite form, and yet it is continually creating forms. It is a mysterious dancing influence, and the only power you have over it is that of shutting it out of your life or allowing it in. But in your relationship with Wonder, anything can emerge. Each person has a unique

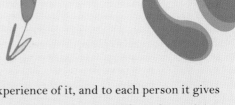

experience of it, and to each person it gives a special knowledge, skills and creativity. Who you really are is discovered in your relationship with that Wonder, and in the way you live that relationship externally.

Of course, these different names refer to your core self. But it becomes a wonder when you experience it.

Finding healing

Lucidity offers several avenues towards physical or psychological healing. To understand how these work and how to find healing, it helps to have a basic picture of human ills, as seen from the point of view of dreams and lucidity.

An analogy of this is electricity going into a house. Electricity is invisible, and by itself it is nothing. It is only when electricity is connected to an appliance, or is earthed, that it is known. Also, electricity can express itself in an amazing number of ways. It can be the power to turn on a washing machine, light, heat, sound, images on a television screen, computer functions, and so on.

Coming back to your body and mind, lucid experience suggests there is a fundamental potential that expresses itself in a variety of ways. First it releases as growth, but it is also cellular activity, sexuality, hunger and digestion, emotions, speech, thinking and perceiving. So, in a sense, things such as speech and sex are simply different ways in which you can

direct this basic energy. The lucid experience of Jon (see page 11) mentioned this energy. He said, 'This sparkling, vibrating energy is life itself and can – if I learn to work with it – grow into any ability or direction that I choose.'

However, problems arise in that what you do, think and feel directs that energy. This happened with Jon – his energy, or experience of himself, had become 'brown and lifeless'. In fact he was suffering from depression, and that disappeared when he

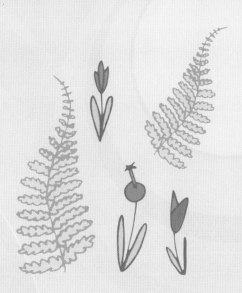

changed his relationship with his life energy. He altered what he was unconsciously creating with the energy of his thoughts and emotions.

UNBLOCKING THE LIFE ENERGY

Problems therefore arise when this flow of life energy, in its various forms, is blocked through repression or pain. It can then become stagnant, or it twists to flow in a destructive manner through negative emotions and thoughts. Des, for instance, whose sexuality had been harmed in childhood, so held this back that it turned into aggression and rage. Tim had watched

his father die from coal dust in his lungs; he had held back from shouting his rage for so long that it became a physical problem in his throat. However, Meg regained the use of her legs after uncovering the resentment she felt about the behaviour of her son.

At a physical level, as we have already seen, you are a river; you are the wind; you are the earth. Taking in polluted water, in the form of factory-made liquids; taking in polluted air, in the form of smoking or living in a dirty environment; taking in lifeless, processed foods – all these degrade your life. So healing is about bringing accord to the attitudes, beliefs and energies that are your life energy. It is about undoing the damage to the river, wind and earth that you are. It is about healing the blindness, paralysis and primal pain that many people experience. But the healing that arises from harmony with your core can also mitigate or heal illnesses connected with viruses, bacteria or physical damage.

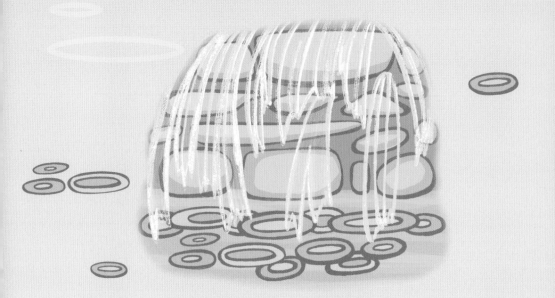

Some of the ways in which you can work towards healing with lucidity are given below.

WORK WITH YOUR DREAMS

Remember that dream images are like icons on a computer. What you do with them connects with the processes underlying the dream. So, while awake, imagine yourself in your dream. Do this by being in the dream and working with the people and creatures in a way to transform your fears and negative emotions into constructive, life-enhancing feelings. Alter the dream in any way that satisfies you, but make sure there are no feelings in you rebelling against the changes. If such

feelings arise, work with them until you resolve the conflict. Work with each dream in this way.

BATHE IN HEALING WATERS

Imagine your core self – your life energy – as a spring of water in which you bathe. As you go to sleep, hold this image in your mind and create a feeling of this flow of life energy permeating your whole being, and relaxing and healing it. Direct this feeling to any part of your body or life that needs healing. Then decide that when you become lucid, you will create this same experience of looking for and finding this flow of living waters from the source of your own existence. Work with what arises

until you can feel the healing change occurring. Repeat this until the healing is apparent in your waking life.

THE POWER OF PLACEBO

Use the powers you have near at hand. The 'placebo effect' is well established as a way of helping or healing serious ills. Everyone has their own power of 'placebo'. To use it, look through your recorded dreams to find those in which a powerful pleasure, uplift or sense of beauty occurs. Use the central image and feeling of such dreams as a meditation. Recreate the pleasure or feelings of well-being. To enhance this, listen to uplifting music read those things that shift your feelings to ones of interest in life and love. Remember that what you feel and believe, or are frightened of, actually creates your inner and outer world.

OPEN TO YOUR CORE

Use the 'seed meditation' described earlier (see page 49). If you have not used it much, practise it until you find a spontaneous experience of it. It is important to create the 'keyboard' condition in which you are ready for the core Life in you to express itself spontaneously as movement, your voice, feelings or imagination. So you should come to the meditation with the condition of 'not knowing' that you practised earlier (see page 69). Then, instead of holding the image of the seed, hold in your mind that you are opening to your core being, from which all that you are arises. You are open to the action of your core and are asking for healing. Let yourself express in any way that arises spontaneously in the meditation. This enables your core to bring about whatever is necessary for your healing.

Using your problem-solving abilities

Solving problems is a basic life skill that you use every day. Most of the time you do it unconsciously – when you look for mislaid keys, or wonder what clothes to wear to deal with today's needs. But sometimes you may feel lost in confronting a situation and require extra help. To do this you can learn to use your problem-solving abilities consciously to find a practical solution.

Lorna, looking for the source of her frustration and tension, describes what she found using lucidity:

I am experiencing an enormous tension throughout my body. I am allowing the tension to rack me, and begin to see what is causing it. It seems to have developed in my childhood. I, like most youngsters, didn't have explained to me what the rules of the game of life are; what the social and biological expectations, regulations, drives and urges are, and how to work with them. But we are supposed to get it right. If you do get this

amazingly complex apparatus of life right, then the bells ring and you are rewarded. Then you climb the social and biological ladder of success. But, if you press the wrong buttons, you slip down the snakes (not up the ladders), as in the game. As I begin to understand this, my tension starts to melt. I am not wrong, I am just learning!

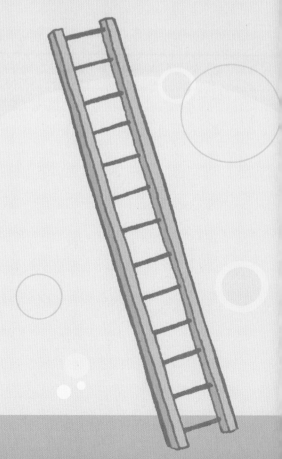

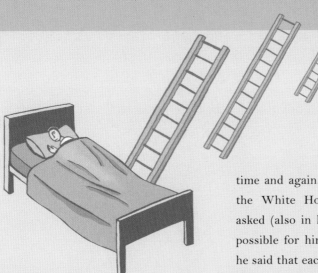

Lorna had never thought of life like that before. She had to leave school at an early age and start work. Nevertheless – like everyone – she had an enormous amount of observed life experience that had never been organized into insights, until she accessed her own problem-solving technique.

And that is fundamentally what lucidity (and this technique) does: it draws from your amazing collection of experience whatever is appropriate to your own situation. But there are other possibilities, too. At times what you access reaches beyond your own experience and knowledge.

While in a sleep state, Edgar Cayce demonstrated this day after day by diagnosing and suggesting cures for people's sicknesses, even though he had never seen them and knew nothing of medicine. His ability to do this was tested time and again. He was even consulted at the White House several times. When asked (also in his sleep state) how it was possible for him to gain such knowledge, he said that each of us connects to what he called a cosmic or universal mind. From this level we can gain information beyond our own learning, although for most of us this is only accessible in sleep.

Dr Harmon Bro made a study of this in his book on psychic experience, and came to the conclusion that such knowledge is open to all of us, and not simply to unique or unusual individuals. Similarly, Dr Karagulla, a neuropsychiatrist who studied this under the name of 'higher sense perception', sees it as a breakthrough to greater creativity. The people she observed were all professionals – businessmen and women, doctors, engineers – using this problem-solving approach to aid them in their work.

STEPS TO GREATER LUCIDITY

Like any other skill, lucidity (in sleeping or waking) needs practice while you are learning it. And it needs to be done one step at a time.

Step 1: thoughts

Thoughts are tools to be used in problem-solving, but are only part of the necessary toolkit. It is important to understand clearly what a thought is, and not to confuse it with any sort of final truth. Any thought or image is only a mental photograph of something or someone. It is never the actual person or thing, and must not be seen as such. As with a photo, thought is only a tiny fragmented copy of what you are considering. Nevertheless, you need to use thoughts in clarifying what it is that you seek an answer to. So write down the essence of what you already understand, and have done, about the problem.

Step 2: the framework

Because you create a world out of your feelings, ideas, beliefs and fears, any negative attitudes that you have can be a massive, self-fashioned wall, shutting off your creative and problem-solving abilities. Review the exercise on opening to your core (see page 67), and check that you can drop any ideas of limitation. You *are not* trying to replace them with ideas of being superhuman; you are simply clearing space. So build a framework of thoughts and feelings that leave you open to further possibilities.

Step 3: going beyond

The 'keyboard' condition has already been used a number of times. However, it needs further definition, as it forms a vital part of problem-solving. Above all, try to bring all of you to the condition. Each part of you is a sense organ. Apart from the five main senses, you also have a sense of balance, a sense of beauty or appropriateness, a sense of sexual attraction or repulsion – and so on, with all your emotions and hungers. Your speech too is expressed out of a subtle sense of things. So your keyboard is all of these – body movement, imagination, emotions, sexual feeling, memory, voice and fantasy – open to responding to your question or problem. It's important that your whole being is open to respond.

GET SOME ANSWERS

Don't think of problem-solving as sitting quietly, thinking. It isn't. You need some level of excitation, motivation and involvement to stimulate it.

1 When you feel that openness and readiness to let your whole being respond to what you are seeking, take this and your question into a lucid dream, using the 'digital watch' approach (see page 52). As you are going to sleep, imagine yourself exploring the question lucidly in a dream.

2 If you do not achieve lucidity, take any dream you have had in response to your question, or take a nightmare (if that is the problem). Walk into the dream, keeping the keyboard condition, and watch what you feel and experience. Ask your question; work with the dream situation, as described earlier.

3 Alternatively (or in addition), use the 'seed meditation' approach (see page 49). But ask your question instead of actually being the seed.

Reaching beyond your limitations

When viewed as a myth, the story of Adam and Eve is a description of an epic change in the evolution of humans. We usually think of evolution in terms of physical change, but huge psychological changes have occurred as well. Humans did not always have self-awareness. Like animals, we were guided by instinct, by an inner sense or innocence. This was in the Garden of Eden, where humanity constantly had access to what we now call the unconscious. Then, with the dawning of self-awareness, came a loss of that innocence, a loss of constant guidance. Only in dreams and trances could humanity now recapture something of that wider knowing or innocence.

In his book *Cosmic Consciousness* (Applewood Books, 2001) Dr Richard Maurice Bucke suggests that we are at present taking the next huge step in evolution: reconnection. Bucke himself experienced what he called 'cosmic consciousness' – a massive influx of intuitive awareness, a leap beyond his usual limitations. Such an experience is a reconnection with the infinite potential underlying our existence.

In the East it has been called enlightenment; I am calling it lucidity; the

early Christians called it the 'pearl of great price', or 'heaven on earth'.

If you have done the previous exercises in this book, you have already been practising some of the most powerful aids towards making this reconnection, towards moving beyond the limitations of self-awareness. Now you need to refine or extend what you have learned. Because your mind and personality have shaped who you are, you need to understand that the shape created so far may not be very flexible or yielding. Your mental and emotional structure might not be capable of taking in huge new vistas of experience. Slow breathing (see page 39) aids this by developing greater strength of will and perseverance. Use it!

WHO AM I?

The next steps help you to go further in looking beyond the surface of things. They are very simple.

1   Take time each day – while walking, riding to work or sitting somewhere – to ask the question: What am I?

2   Make this a fascinated enquiry, without any struggle. Take into the question other questions, such as: Am I my head? Am I one of my limbs? Am I my thoughts? Am I my emotions? Am I what other people think of me, or tell me I am?

3   With each of these questions, follow it through. For instance, you might lose a limb and still feel that you exist as a person. So who are you essentially? If you are not essentially a limb, how does that connect with your physical characteristics?

4   Carry it further still: consider who you are and can be in your dreams – what does that suggest about what you are?

5   When you have a sense of the power and range of this question, take it into a lucid dream and explore it.

Remembering your deep history

Lucidity is not a sport or a thrilling roller-coaster ride. It isn't something you have a quick thrill with, and then leave behind. You are gradually meeting yourself more and more fully. This includes the slow uncovering of your history. And your history did not begin with your conception and birth. Any brief study of history reveals that the present shape of cities, countryside, national characteristics, cultural attitudes and beliefs developed from past events and people. Similarly, your own attitudes and patterns of behaviour did not originate with your birth and childhood experiences.

In his forties Roger had a short dream that he didn't think had much in it. But on exploring it, he uncovered the roots of a lifelong social attitude that had plagued him. It became clear, as he went deeper into his unconscious, that his father had passed this on to him, and it had come down through the generations for hundreds of years, from a time of political and religious persecution.

Your present personality has its roots in the distant past. This is not referring particularly to reincarnation – that is just a word. It means observable traits, which if you trace them back have their origins in a past prior to your birth. But of course your deep history is also the memory of your own development and the turns it took from conception onwards. This remembering also puts you in touch with what can be called your destiny. You bring from your connection with the past (and from your childhood) a sense of important things to do or learn in your lifetime. Satisfying this innate drive brings tremendous satisfaction.

You can think of who you are as a snowball that has rolled down a hill and gathered more and more snow as it rolled. The snow gathered in the past is still with you; it is not

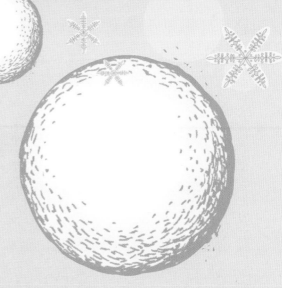

left behind. Becoming aware of the part it plays in the present has probably already begun, in remembering and recording your dreams. This is because dreams are like that snowball – in expressing who you are, they incorporate your past.

PROMOTE RECALL

Recalling your deep history happens spontaneously as you extend your lucidity. However, you can help it to occur in the following way:

1 Start by using the relaxation techniques (see pages 32–33) prior to going to sleep.

2 When you are relaxed, open to your core (see page 67).

3 Then imagine your body as it is in sleep; visualize yourself as you are in sleep. This doesn't have to be exact, but try to gain a sense of your body, if you can.

4 Now imagine that your awareness is leaving your sleeping body and flying high up in the sky. But the sky you are flying in is the upper regions of the landscape of your life. You are going high enough to have a view over the entire span of your life and, in doing so, gaining that oversight into who you are and where you come from.

5 Sleep and carry this image into a lucid or normal dream.

Touching ecstasy

Ecstatic pleasure sometimes arises from a life-changing event, or a wonderful sexual experience. Unfortunately these things are quick to pass away. However, when all else falls away, there is an unconditional bliss at the core of you. Usually you fail to experience it, because your thoughts and emotions are so noisy and you identify with them so fully. But when you let go of them sufficiently, when they are silenced (as can occur in deep relaxation), the ocean of unchanging bliss is uncovered.

An ancient Tibetan teaching about finding this unconditional bliss says that you must cease all activity. It goes on to say that the activity to avoid is the disordered activity of the mind, which constantly – like a builder erecting ideas – creates an imaginary world in which it shuts itself like a chrysalis in its cocoon.

This goes back to the process you are learning from your dream-watching – that you constantly create a full-surround virtual reality that you take to be real. You believe its reality when you have a beautiful dream, but also when an evil darkness threatens you. But they are both your own creations. There are two ways in which you can touch ecstasy.

HOW TO SHAPE EXPERIENCE

With each dream you recall, ask yourself out of what hopes, fears, pains or life experiences you have created it. Recognize that the dream in some way depicts the ever-shifting world of your own mind, emotions and sexuality. It portrays at times the deep, surging processes of your life energy as it strives to survive, grow and find satisfaction. That life energy is like water, and can take on any shape. Your fears and hopes, beliefs and convictions, mould it into certain emotions and experiences. Unwittingly you shape it into pleasure or pain. Your aim in watching your dreams is

to consider how you shape your own experience. There is no need to attempt to interpret your dreams – just see how you live in a cocoon of your own making. This alone moves you towards the freedom that removes many ills.

OPENING TO YOUR CORE

Use the slow breathing exercise (see page 38) to quieten your body and mind. After some minutes, when you reach this quietness, use the relaxation techniques (see pages 32–33), discarding all physical tension and thoughts. Literally give up, if you can, and maintain awareness until you slip into the borderland of sleep. If your thoughts catch hold of you and drag you off, repeat over and over again to yourself while continuing to drop all tension, 'I am letting go of my thoughts and feelings. I am dropping all effort and sinking into sleep with awareness, opening to my core.'

Remember you already have that bliss as the basic level of your existence. I believe the Big Bang sent out a huge vibratory sound that still echoes throughout all things, giving them existence – just as sand on glass takes shape from a musical note. It echoes within us as bliss.

Transforming worn-out habits

William James, a psychologist, philosopher and brother of the American writer Henry James, said that the only difference between a hardened criminal and a socially successful person is habits.

Once, while on a small local beach with his children and dog, Ted had fun clearing the debris brought in by winter storms, and built a bonfire with it. Some of the debris consisted of aerosol cans. So he got the children to stand behind a large rock, then threw the cans onto the fire one at a time. After the third dramatic explosion his dog ran frantically from behind the rock and headed home – at least a mile away. Three years later Ted, his wife and dog were on the same beach sunbathing. They had been there for hours, but as the sun sank, Ted stood up and leaned on that same large rock. Suddenly the dog looked at him strangely, turned and was gone. This is a dramatic example of how

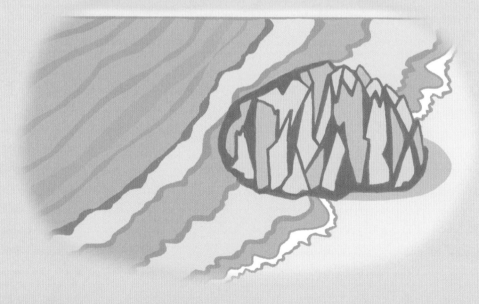

habitual responses can be etched deeply into animals. Fortunately, unlike Ted's dog, we can re-evaluate the fear or urgency that we feel to repeat original responses. Unfortunately, we often fail to realize the nature of what is happening to us.

AWARENESS OF NEGATIVE HABITS

Humans would not be able to walk or talk without the amazing support of our habits. But some habits – like repeatedly choosing a destructive lover; constantly feeling inferior; destroying opportunities; or mishandling authority figures – are more undermining than supportive. The more lucid we become, the more we become aware of these negative habits and their roots. This in itself transforms them to some degree, but we can also speed up the process. For instance, our humanness is built on a much older animal self, which still has its natural ways of responding to pain and anxiety. Just like Ted's dog, if something frightens you, you will react.

I once had to return to a house in which I had experienced months of emotional anguish. As we were driving there, I felt great stomach pains. I thought at first that I had eaten something poisonous. But then I asked my unconscious what the problem was. Immediately the response came, 'You are taking me back to that house where I was hurt.' I realized I was dealing with my animal self, so I talked to it, just as I would a horse or dog. 'Steady. We are not staying there long, and the things that hurt are no longer there.' Immediately the pain began to recede and the visit was easily achieved.

ASK YOUR DREAMS FOR HELP

Try to understand the dynamics of your response. If it is not easy to find clarity, look to your dreams for help. Ask for a guiding dream, or go into a lucid dream and seek the cause. For instance, a radio researcher was offered the job of presenter, but was on the verge of refusing. She dreamed that an air-raid attack was taking place and that she jumped into a ditch to hide. From the dream she realized that she was scared of being out in the open – in public view and possible criticism. This enabled her to deal with her anxiety. When you clarify the situation, take time to talk to yourself as if to a child or animal. Explain why the reaction takes place, and offer a way of moving beyond it.

LOOK FOR THEMES

Carefully look through your dream journal and make a note of recurring themes. Possible themes are: love – satisfying or otherwise; looking for something; running to or from something; trying to find your way; hiding; being trapped; starting something; building or renovating; a relationship; being with others; being alone; leaving things or people behind; death; birth; growth; fear; digging; and so on. Take one theme at a time and work with each of the dreams expressing that theme. Its recurrence suggests that a habitual response is involved. So imagine yourself in the dream and create a different ending. Rework the dream so it is more satisfying. For instance, if you are always passive in your dreams, imagine yourself being more dynamic and forceful. If you

always relate to unsatisfactory men or women, change the dream to one where you gain satisfaction. Carry on until you see a shift in the dreams you experience while asleep. Aim to become lucid in each of the dream themes and search for the roots of the habit and ways to change it.

THE MIRROR OF AWARENESS

This next technique is life-changing, but it has to be done so frequently that it becomes a habit, active in the background of your waking and sleeping life. If you do not have time for the other approaches, use this one. Start by imagining there is a mirror within you. This mirror is your awareness or consciousness. The things you think or feel are images that pass across that mirror and for a while have existence in it, but they all shift and go. Only the mirror remains. When this is fairly clear, sit and watch what is in the mirror of your awareness. Notice whether it is a thought, a feeling, a body sensation or a memory. Give each one an identity, such as: 'This is an opinion', 'This is a thought', 'This is an emotion', 'This is from something I read', 'This is a conjecture about an experience', and so on. As you get used to this, imagine standing in the midst of your dreams. Use one dream at a time. Hold on to the sense of your naked awareness being something beyond the images that play upon the mirror. As you review each dream, say to yourself, 'These dream people and images depict passing emotions and thoughts. I will realize this while I sleep and transform frightening or unsatisfying dreams. I will remember myself as the shining mirror.'

Finding greater sexual and emotional fulfilment

Dreams can portray sex as something greater than mere genital movements or sensations. Genital sex is simply the first stage of sexuality or mating. It is one way of expressing the incredible flow of life. To mate fully is to merge fully.

Dreams suggest that what is called love in today's world is often a form of childhood dependence. This seems obvious from the enormous pain that broken relationships bring to many people. So the movement towards a greater love, to which dreams try to take you, means clearing out the many childhood pains, angers and fears that cloud your present attempts at loving relationships.

Also, before you can adequately love another, you must achieve a male–female unity within yourself. This does not mean that a man should try outwardly to be a woman, or a woman should try outwardly to be a man. It means gradually managing full unity with the opposite gender in your dream life. If you have not managed that, you constantly seek yourself in another person and are likely to be disappointed – and maybe even betrayed. Two dreams illustrate this:

• The dreamer is standing at the door of a Quaker Meeting House with his bride-to-be. Someone at the door asks for their tickets to enter. The bridegroom doesn't have one, so his bride goes in and he can't.

• The dreamer knows an alien, whom he loves. The love is so intense that they give themselves to each other, to the point where he absorbs her personality with all its memories, and she absorbs his. This feels like a very important thing to do.

In the first example the dreamer hasn't got the 'ticket' – meaning the quality needed to wed fully. He hasn't yet achieved male-female unity within himself. In the second example the same dreamer achieves this; it happens with an alien, because he was previously alienated from this love and wholeness. After this dream he found many people spontaneously approaching him, both with and for love.

LOVE YOURSELF TO LOVE ANOTHER

If you can learn to love yourself properly, you will be able to give yourself to others.

1   In every dream (lucid or otherwise) attempt as full a relationship as possible with each person or animal in that dream.

2   Hold the idea that everything in the dream is an aspect of yourself, and you will come to wholeness as you integrate each part. Obviously this is not a rule without exception, as there may be some parts you want to discard. But in general move towards integration.

3   Do this in your dream, in lucidity, or while awake through visualization.

Keith describes a beautiful dream that illustrates one possible result:

A woman led me rather reluctantly into a large building. Inside, along a passage, a mesh of patterned energy completely filled the space. With no hesitation, the woman and I walked into this energy. We knew we would be absorbed and become wholly a part of this life form. I could feel the energy totally penetrate me and work on me in a healing way that was transforming me. I knew I was being made whole.

Travelling in time and space

The theory of the Big Bang suggests an event from which time and space emerged. Prior to that, there was no universe, no time and no space. This is an incredible concept, and if you are in the business of tracing your origins, the Big Bang lies behind the existence of us all. Science has explored it using radio telescopes and measuring radiation and light shifts, but in some ways it is shown only as a physical phenomenon. In fact, our present cultural and philosophical views often leave us with the idea that we are basically just a physical body with a mysterious and inexplicable self-awareness. As David Bowie said in one of his songs, 'Life's a bitch – and then you die.'

However, the exploration of our origins has been undertaken for thousands of years as an inward journey using lucidity to cross the frontier of consciousness. Hindu explorers described the expansion of the universe ages before the arrival of modern rational science. They also pointed out that it expands and contracts in cycles. But they added an equation that only the latest exponents of new physics mention: consciousness. They say that the universe has Sat-Chit-Ananda – Being-Consciousness-Bliss – to its very foundations. Each of us, according to our talent and determination, can discover this for ourselves.

BEING BOTH HERE AND THERE

However, such exploration of time and space is not solely the territory of past seers. Sir Auckland Geddes, surgeon and one-time British ambassador to the US, gives a brilliant description of a lucid experience, showing how time and space are no longer the same in the lucid condition. Becoming suddenly and violently ill with gastroenteritis, he quickly became unable to move or phone for help. As this was occurring he noticed two levels of awareness. One was normal sensory awareness in his body; the other was external to his body. From the external self he could see not only his body, but also his house, garden and surroundings. He needed only to think of a friend or place, and immediately he was there, and was later able to verify what he saw. In looking at his body, he noticed that the brain was only an end-organ, like a condensing plate, upon which memory and awareness played. The mind, he said, was not in the brain; rather, the brain was in the mind, like a radio in the play of signals. He then observed his daughter come in and discover his condition, saw her telephone a doctor friend, and saw the doctor at the same time. His observation was that in the lucid condition we can be 'here' and 'there' simultaneously.

There is even more to this ability, though. Stefan could move backwards in time and could experience the past as if he were there, living it. His ability to do this was so accurate that he was employed by a professor at the University of Warsaw to describe the origins of ancient archaeological finds. As he explored each object, the room Stefan was in would fade away and he would 'live' in the past of the object and see its surroundings.

Whole books have been written about these amazing abilities and their reality. Notable among them are *Breakthrough to*

Creativity (DeVorss, 1991) by pioneering physician and neuropsychiatrist Shafica Karagulla, and *The Holographic Universe* (HarperCollins, 1996) by Michael Talbot, summarizing the work of leading physicist David Bohm and neurophysiologist Karl Pribram. Although the higher levels of moving through time and space are usually shown only by people who use such skills as part of their work (some doctors, for instance), most people can reach beyond the limitations of their body senses and travel in space and time. In fact, this is fundamental to knowing who you are, although, as with any skill, it needs practice and perseverance to draw it out of you.

TO INFINITY AND BEYOND

Prepare yourself for your travels by gaining as clear a sense as possible that time and space as you know them in your body are not the same as in lucid dreaming. Trust the fact that you are a native of the inner world, through your years of exploring it unconsciously in dreams. But remember that the world you meet reflects what you and others create from your thoughts, attitudes, fears and emotions.

1 The first step is recognition of your place in the scheme of things. Just as the skipper of a sailing boat can choose a direction, but has to recognize that it is the wind that gives him power, so you must recognize that success depends on the greater energies of the ocean of mind in which you are immersed, and how you relate to them. If there is no 'wind', you are unable to move.

2 Your success depends not upon your will or worldly power, but on the way you relate to the intelligences and energies that constitute your being – shown in your dreams as animals,

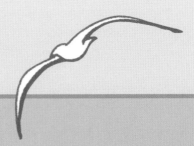

people and natural phenomena such as trees and rivers. Success also depends upon your motivation. So an urgent and deeply felt request has more chance than a desire to experiment.

3 Imagination or visualization using imagery is the language of the unconscious. Use it to form your request for whatever you want to experience. Put this as a fervent desire to your core self. Watch your dreams to see how you might be blocking the way to its fulfillment.

4 The possibilities are endless. In lucidity you can visit any place on Earth; you can talk with or develop a relationship with any person, living or dead; explore the past or glimpse the forming of the future; uncover your past beyond this latest birth, and in doing so understand the life lessons and work that you are meeting in this life.

5 Write down your request – such as travelling to a distant place – on a piece of paper that you can carry in your hand. Hold it in your hand at times and read it, visualizing success. Use the digital watch method (see page 52) to induce lucidity, and go to sleep with the written request in your hand.

DREAMING: THE MIRACLE OF TRANSFORMATION

The transforming influence of dreams

Imagine living in a house with only one window and one door. The door leads onto a busy road, and the window looks out onto a park with trees. Now imagine you wake up one morning to find you have six doors and 20 windows, and each one leads to something different. You can now look at a beautiful seashore, a mountain range, a desert, and walk out into different parts of the world. A crazy idea perhaps, but not if you're acquainted with your dreams. They are windows and doorways to an infinite number of experiences and insights.

However, dreams appear to give back what you believe they are capable of. At one period of my life I had been exploring a method of entering the lucid state while awake. I had read a great deal about past cultures and modern psychology and psychiatry, so I already had wide-ranging expectations of what might be possible. Consequently, I found my experiences very rich and transforming. However, when I joined a group who were using the same practice, but had a much narrower view of what was possible I discovered that their

range of experience matched their restricted expectations.

When you look at one of your dreams and try to understand it, in a way you are approaching a wonderful alien – an alien with intelligence and powers that perhaps you cannot even conceive of at the moment. Here are some points to ponder and use in relating to your dreams.

ASK FOR HELP

Dreams arise from a different type of awareness and intelligence than your waking self. Like any intelligent being, your dream will respond to you. If you don't understand its message, tell it so. Ask it for help or a clearer message. Challenge your dreams to show you what they are capable of. Ask them to widen your horizons.

PERSIST IN YOUR ATTEMPTS

A dream is a sort of baby language the dream maker uses to try to reduce its message to your level of awareness. It is couched in imagery or mime. If you persist in trying to enter into this communication, you will eventually break through to the enormity of awareness from which the dream is communicating.

IMAGINE YOURSELF IN THE DREAM

To understand a dream more fully, sit and use the relaxation techniques (see pages 32–33), then imagine yourself as one of the characters, animals or places in your dream. Literally fill their shape with your awareness – become them or it – and watch the screen of your body–mind to see what it feels like. Let your feelings and imagination respond. Don't worry if it is 'true' or not. If it works in your life, it is true. Put what you experience into words and do the same with each part of your dream. It can help to 'be' the dream character in the 'keyboard' condition, and to allow full body/feeling response as in the seed meditation (see page 49).

Bringing the new you into everyday reality

One of the biggest hurdles to cross in becoming lucid is realizing clearly that whatever you believe – whatever you think, fear or accept as real – you begin to live and create in your life. The other hurdle is that some of the difficulties are there from the beginning. Perhaps they have shaped your life in particular ways, and now you are faced with the task of trying to transform inner problems or anxieties.

At a period when Mary was feeling deeply frustrated with her situation, she sought some advice using a few of the techniques explained earlier. The response was extraordinarily clear, like someone gently explaining how to deal with her problems. To quote what was said:

Because you make real what you believe, you are in a trap of your own creation. It is not as if somebody else can take it away from you. It is no good appealing to God to remove it, because it is you who have the power of creating or recreating it. You made this trap. You

have to find the combination yourself and undo it. To put it simply, if you believe life has no meaning, then you are living a life with no meaning. You are creating your own limitations. If you live a belief that you have wider possibilities – even if that belief is only that you have a right to talk to your neighbour, then perhaps you will go to them and say, 'Can I have a spoonful of sugar?' You will then have stepped beyond your previous limitations. Each such tiny step creates a wider life. So who knows where the boundaries are? Who knows where you will travel to, if you dare to take the next small step?

That is one of the great secrets: taking the next small step. You don't have to be superhuman, and everyday life offers you the opportunity to transform. As you reach out to life, so life reaches out to you – and 'life' includes plants, animals, children and people of all nations. It includes the rain and sunshine, the sky and rivers. Believe me, this is not simply a platitude. Lucidity offers an incredibly powerful way of transforming who you are and of bringing positive change into your life. It offers everything from deep healing of childhood trauma, to creating your future by forming it in your mind and your lucid dreams first.

PRACTISING YOUR DREAMS

The small steps you can take, which build into big changes, involve practising what you find in your dreams. As an example, Ryan dreamed that he was making repairs in a house he had lived in. He was mending an electric meter, and needed to screw something from the bottom. He leaned forward to apply more pressure and, as he did so, looked down and saw that he was balanced on a stool, which was in turn balanced on two other stools. He started to

fall, but became lucid and realized that he could not fall, so he was suspended there and finished the job.

Ryan described the house as one he had renovated with his wife, and related it to satisfying changes he was making in his life. The stools were actual ones he had known in his first marriage, in which he constantly felt unable to make positive changes. So he saw them as fears that his present, positive moves would collapse. But what he found in lucidity showed him that he was not at the mercy of his anxieties any more. And the meter represented his flow of greater energy arising from his new awareness. So Ryan practised his move from anxiety to confidence, until it became a part of his everyday outlook.

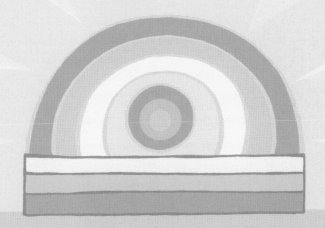

CREATE A NEW YOU

Try using your own dreams to create a new attitude within yourself.

1 See if you can find in your dreams and lucidity an example of either failing or succeeding in a particular direction, or running away from or dealing with a threat or problem.

2 If the dream is one of success, practise the stance or quality that enables you to succeed. If the dream is one of failure, try out different attitudes or responses until you find one that makes a difference, then use it in your waking life.

3 Write everything down to secure it in your memory.

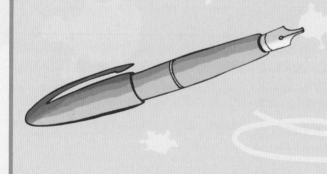

Recently a friend asked for help in facing a difficult change after she lost her job. She described the image she had of her situation as that of being alone and stuck high up in a cable car. When asked what or who could help change the situation, she said the only figure that came to mind was Superman: he got the car moving and her mood subsequently shifted. It doesn't matter if what you come up with seems like pure fantasy – if it shifts your feelings, it has value. Remember that you are much bigger, and with greater resources, than you believe.

SUMMON YOUR DREAM CHARACTERS

There is another immense resource in your dreams. If you look through your journal you will notice a wide variety of characters, animals and places. The more dreams you have, the greater the variety is likely to be. Each of these is an expression of your own resources, your own talent and your own potential. The fact that they appear as external simply says that you have not yet fully identified with or claimed those parts of you. So when you are problem-solving, when you are looking for that extra zest in creativity or courage in dealing with a particular situation, call on your dream characters for help.

1   Start by listing your main dream characters, animals and places, then add a brief description of what their abilities or talents are, or what qualities they bring you.

2   Delve into them to discover this, by imagining yourself as them. Role-play and find out who or what they are. Identify with the character or place and discover its secrets. Whether peaceful or aggressive, wise or energetic, these are all parts of your potential.

3   Call on them when you need to. Do this by seeking their help in a situation of danger, or if you are being attacked in a dream or facing fear.

Levels of experience in the new frontier

The five levels of awareness were described earlier (see pages 56–57). Now let us look at some of those levels when they are met as personal experience.

LEVEL 2: DREAMING

Dreams are the level that most of us know best, and the main factors of this level are that you experience yourself in a full-surround virtual reality. Humans are used to recognizing symbols, such as a red cross to represent a humanitarian organization; such a symbol links with all aspects of that organization, so it may be enormously wide in its associations. However, we are less expert at realizing and recognizing that a person, an animal or a place in a dream can also depict a mass of our experience. The drama or events of a dream are a multi-dimensional expression of your personality, of its many facets – sexuality, ambition, fear, and so on – and of the way in which you relate to life events.

No computer (however amazing its functions) can yet do what your mind does in creating a dream. It produces an entity, such as a dream character, that can have a conversation with you and, in so doing, draw spontaneously on huge areas of your experience or memories. Behind the image lie vast amounts of data, emotional response and created patterns of behaviour. So the main thing to remember at this level is that you are in a full-surround data-bank of fantastic information. You can tap this information just as you would tap any person, by asking questions and prodding it for a response. Even the trees and animals in your dreams are enormous reservoirs of information, linking back – perhaps infinitely – with your potential, experience and core.

LEVEL 3: BEYOND THE IMAGES OF DREAMS

Generally you are lost in or carried along by your dreams. But when you gain lucidity (either in a dream or while awake), you can penetrate the surface of the dream images. This takes you to the next level, in which you become aware of, and can work with, the enormity of who you are.

In most cases you will probably be confronted by 'housework' or 'renovation' that needs to be done. This is the clearing or healing of the many blocks, fears and pains that you have gathered from conception onwards – or even from the distant past – and which act as obstacles in your path to a fuller, healthier and happier experience of living. However, the process is not simply one of healing or cleansing; it is also one of learning. This is because, if the work is done well, you will gradually remember your history – recovering your childhood, infancy and even life in the womb. At times you will also remember your 'life in eternity': an experience of the timeless core of you that has dipped into life again and again. At that point you will realize something of the main life lessons that you are learning (or trying to learn) as your present personality. When that happens you will know your part in the eternal quest that is life.

Using your intuition

Intuition is one of the most formidable life tools when you learn to use it with skill. But to do this you need to develop discrimination and perception. Do so by always testing your intuition against what is observable and what actually works.

Everyone uses intuition throughout the day. In fact you use intuition more often than your reasoning ability. Most decisions you arrive at, and the responses you make, arise from collected experience and from subliminal impressions of the situation or person that you face. It would take too long to reason out carefully each thing you do. So you arrive at an intuitive response from gathered experience, which has not all been made conscious. This experience might be a special area of study, such as medicine, engineering or working with animals; or it might be more general, such as the everyday life experience of people and social interactions. This form of

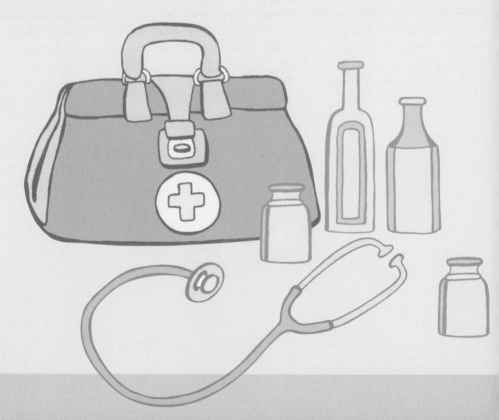

intuition can be examined afterwards, and with time the sources of it can be explained or understood.

Intuition can also come from cues given to you by other people in their behaviour, facial expressions, clothing, speech and tones, posture and movements. You gather an enormous amount of information about other people within a few seconds of meeting them.

For most people, intuition or hunches occur spontaneously or without real awareness. To take hold of the process and use it consciously changes it into an enormous life skill. It is not an exaggeration to say that when you hone your intuition, there is almost nothing it cannot investigate. Some of the greatest scientific discoveries were made by intuitive leaps – especially in lucid dreams. Some of the finest literature and arts developed from an intuitive vision of things. Doctors and counsellors who are skilled in using intuition employ it every day in their work.

However, an intuitive feeling or response can come from many sources, so you need to train your powers of observation to discern whether what you are encountering is an anxiety, an expression of prejudice or old beliefs and opinions, or whether it comes from acute perception of the situation. As you train your intuition, you can direct it to express itself as images, as a clear perception of something, or even as what I call a 'spontaneous voice'. True skill comes from repeated practice.

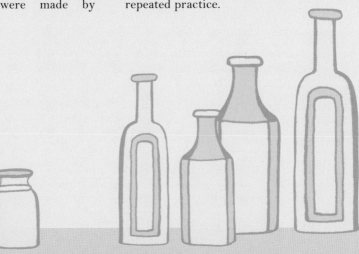

DEVELOP YOUR OWN INTUITION

The prime skill required in consciously using your intuition is that of being able to take on the 'keyboard' condition. In this way you learn to observe the subtle changes in the different sensory areas of yourself: physical sensations; movement; mime; sexual responses; emotions; imagination; memory, vocalization and fantasy. These are all ways in which your intuitive sense can express itself. The three main methods to use are as follows:

Method 1

1   Clarify the question into which you seek insight. You should have one single issue in mind (not several questions in one). It might be a direct question such as: What should I guard against? What direction should I take? What sort of relationship can I expect from my new lover?

2   When you have defined your question, take it into sleep in order to incubate a dream or lucid state so that you can explore the question. Write it on a piece of paper and keep this in your hand, looking at it until you develop a habit that can be carried over into sleep. Imagine looking at the paper in your hand while you are dreaming. As you go to sleep, take on the 'keyboard' condition and continue to hold your paper in your hand.

3   Carefully record any dreams and explore them for the answer to and insight into your question.

Method 2

1   Sit somewhere you can be quiet for about 10–15 minutes.

2   Open to your core (see page 67). Relax into that and take on the mental state of relaxed observation described in the exercise entitled 'What did you dream' (see page 35).

3   Now ask your question and watch the flow of memories, of fantasy, and any shifts in body sensations. What you are

attempting to do is not simply think about this, for thinking usually only runs over the same old ideas again and again. Your open watching enables impressions, imagination and intuition to arise from deeper or wider sources. Sometimes the answer will not come until you have given up watching.

Method 3

1 This is similar to the above method, but has many more possibilities. Again open to your core (see page 67).

2 This time stand and use the carving in space exercise (see page 37). When your body (and perhaps your voice) is expressing spontaneously, ask your specific question.

3 Allow time for the answer to be expressed in mime, in posture, in your voice or in the imagery and direct experiences that can arise from this particular approach.

TESTING YOUR CORE SELF

Your core self is not interested in trivial pursuits – it is the wonder and miracle that grew you from conception. However, it is completely involved in your life and experience. It is constantly trying to find ways to help your unfoldment. So go to it with your questions. Practise until a good dialogue develops. Test the accuracy of what emerges.

Although I have not found the core self to lie, people often take what arises and interpret it according to their own desires or longings. What appears might have arisen from anxieties and simply be an expression of these. That is not a lie – just a representation of what you hold within you. So develop self-observation and discrimination when using your intuition. In particular, explore the carving in space exercise, because it holds so much potential. It is a way of learning how to allow more of yourself to express spontaneously and therefore permit fuller responses from your core, and it is always readily available.

Exploring worlds beyond your senses

Everything you see around you has a hidden nature – hidden, that is, to your physical senses. The people you are with have their own thoughts and feelings. They have a condition of health (or otherwise) in their body and mind. They have a history that is written in their memories, their physical posture and their body condition. These things are visible to you when you use senses other than simply your eyes and ears. Louise relates the following story:

While working at a hotel, cleaning a bench, I was idly listening to the boss and one of the female employees. They were talking about customers, and how trade had been. Then I glanced up at them and suddenly my whole perception changed. Every tiny movement of their hands, limbs, bodies and faces was pouring out information to me. Every expression, every tone and shift of voice was understood in a way I had never experienced before. I could 'see' that these two people had at some time been sexually involved. I also saw that this involvement had created a column of
energy passing between them, through which they were communicating with each other unconsciously. I later asked the woman if she had in fact been involved sexually with the boss, and she smiled and said yes.

That is simply one tiny part of what you can 'see' when your other sensory perceptions are working. And it has nothing to do with weird spirits, sorcery or magic. What happened to Louise was that she became aware of a level of perception within her that everyone possesses. It is an awareness of body language, which animals developed over millions of years and which we still have within us, although it seldom breaks through humans' 'civilized' training and thinking mind.

We have other senses, too. A recent feature in *New Scientist* magazine told the story of Erik, who lost his sight at 13, but now (20 years on) can 'see' with his tongue. A researcher at Wisconsin Medical School developed a means by which tiny electronic impulses from a video camera were fed to a small device, which in turn sent them to

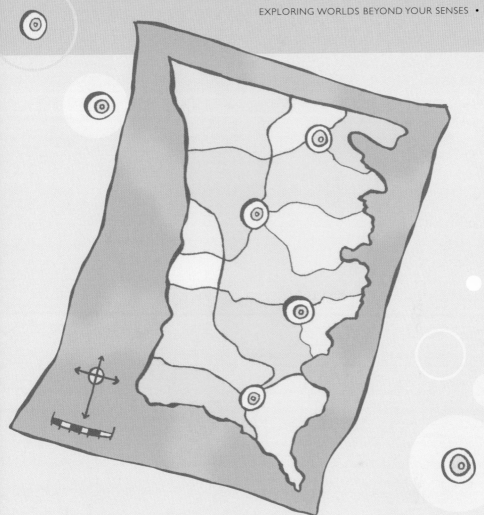

Erik's tongue. Erik's brain – completely at ease with translating nerve impulses from the eye into visual impressions – translated the impulses from his tongue in the same way, enabling him to see.

DOORWAYS OUT OF YOUR IMMEDIATE WORLD

The point is that whatever the impulses, signals or vibrations, the human brain is adept at forming them into imagery or experience that we can understand. Just as dreams turn physical and emotional conditions that were previously unconscious into dramatic, full-surround virtual reality, so we can do the same with other sources of energy. However, until recently we lived in a mental and social environment that told us this was impossible. As I have already mentioned, our beliefs create their own reality. We therefore live within a small world of our

own making. Here, I am attempting to show you doorways out of it.

There are, of course, other reasons why you might not be experiencing the world as fully as you are capable. You might not *want* to see what is going on around or within you. You may have shut down those other levels of perception in childhood so that you could appear 'normal'. It might even be that you are a prisoner of the massive collective consciousness in which you exist. The commercial powers of society bombard us with a view of the world encouraging us to feel incomplete and therefore be consumers. Part of this barrage tells us that life is meaningless, or we are helpless sinners and live within enormous limitations.

There is a powerful current flowing towards waking up – calling you to go beyond your limitations – and you can step into that current. There are several ways to do this. You have already developed the early stages of this awareness in previous exercises and techniques. Here are two methods to take you even further.

OPEN YOURSELF

You need an open door within, to enable a sense of what surrounds you to enter. One way to do this is to think of yourself as a TV screen that you are watching. Observe what body changes, shift of feelings, ideas or images occur when you ask what is hidden from your normal senses in what you are looking at. You need to be focused and quiet inside before this can happen, this is where your practice of slow breathing (see page 39) and opening to your core (see page 67) will come in. Practise on an item that belongs to someone else – something they have had a lot of contact with, such as a ring or a pen. Think of it as bearing messages, much as a CD does. Hold it and use your body and mind as a screen on which the messages can play. Practise until you begin to recognize and understand what you receive.

ENLARGE YOUR WORLD

Being lucid in your dreams is itself an enlargement of your world. But often it only reflects what you believe, or the skills you have developed in your waking activities. This is why you need to develop other skills that are transferable into your lucid experience. This next skill is designed to do this. It involves developing the habit, when you are looking at people or natural objects, of wondering what their inner world is like. If you could pictorially see or experience in some way what it is like to be a tree or a particular person, what would you find? Look at people and observe what images or feelings arise. Learn to distinguish between what are impressions and what are your own feelings. Clear your mind and disconnect when you have finished.

You live in the midst of an extraordinary universe. What you see of it through your physical senses is only the tiniest fragment of what is there. So take time to listen to your wider awareness, and to the strange and wonderful beauty and wisdom it unveils.

The creative leap: lucidity without sleep

In January 1972 two friends and I formed an experimental group. We wanted to explore the possibility of the dream process breaking through into waking consciousness, with ourselves as the subjects. Our main motivation at that time was to see whether the healing functions of dreaming could be more fully exploited. I, for one, was seeking personal healing from depression and psychosomatic pain.

Franz Mesmer, the father of modern hypnotism, found that when he placed subjects in a relaxed condition they experienced spontaneous movements, powerful fantasies, vocalization and the healing of trauma. I realized that all of these connected with the dream process. Having watched humans and animals move while dreaming, I theorized that during a dream the movements being experienced only partially express themselves through the body. Because dreaming is largely an attempt to bring the body and mind to balance and growth, I thought that if we could catalyze a process of dreaming while awake, and these movements were fully permitted, we could greatly enhance this process. My reading about different world cultures suggested that this process had been used many times, in many different ways, in the past.

Our experimental group developed enormously, and for me at least represented an extraordinary introduction to waking lucidity and the exploration of what was usually unconscious. I also found healing of the pain and depression I had been experiencing.

YOUR GURU, THE BODY

Your body has arisen from living cells that are as old as life on this planet. Your body, mind, emotions and imagination are the screen upon which ancient life can project its wisdom and experience. What arises from the ocean of mind within you depends on who you are, what you need (not necessarily what you want) and what you seek.

1   Your connection with your core has deepened through your use of the different exercises in this book. Now go back to the exercises on carving in space (see page 37) and the dried seed meditation (page 49) and use them again.

2   This time approach the exercises with greater awareness of opening to your core. Keep the 'keyboard' condition in place as you do the exercises, be ready to go deeper than you have in the past.

3   You can either approach these exercises expecting your inner process to bring to you whatever it knows you need, or perhaps with a specific question or request.

THE WAKING LUCID DREAM

You will need 20–30 minutes to complete this exercise.

1 Find a comfortable place in which you will not be disturbed and where your body is at ease, with your head supported in some way.

2 Make a tape of the following steps, if you can, so that you can listen to it without having to look at this book.

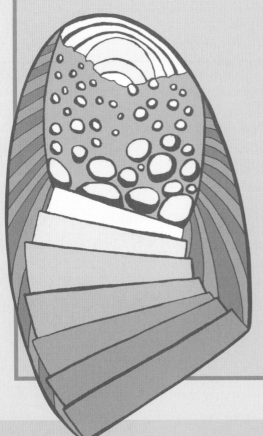

3 First, slow down by practising slow breathing (see page 39) for a minute or two, dropping any tension from your face and anus, as recommended. Say to yourself mentally, 'My thoughts and emotions are gradually becoming quiet. They are melting away like snow in the sun. Without effort they are melting away. As this is happening I am seeing myself in a house. It is a house I love and am at ease in. It is the house of my own body and mind, and I am going more deeply into it than ever before.' Repeat this.

4 Now you will see a door on your left. Open the door and you will see steps leading downwards into a rocky, but illuminated tunnel. This is the tunnel you usually descend in sleep. However, now you are descending into a state of sleep while remaining aware of what you are experiencing.

5 Go down seven steps. See and feel yourself doing this. Count the steps. At the bottom there is a stream. It is warm and you undress and bathe in it, washing away the influences of your waking life. Cross the stream, and there

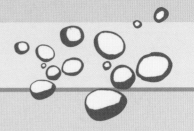

are some robes you can choose to wear. Put on whatever colour of robe you wish.

6 Now go down another seven steps to a deeper level. Count the steps. At the bottom there is another door. Pause before the door and say to yourself, 'When I pass through this door, I enter the greater mind and life within me. I have left behind the limitations of my waking life.'

7 Now pass through the door, and you will see yourself standing on the bright shore of an infinite ocean. Behind you in a rock face is the door you just came through. It is blue. Stand for a while on the edge of the ocean and feel yourself filled and penetrated by the peace and energy of what you are meeting.

8 In this place you can ask for healing; you can ask for wisdom regarding something that is troubling or perplexing you. Do not be concerned if you still feel awake and aware of what is happening in the external world. That is not a problem, as long as you keep gently watching the screen of your body–mind. In this way you will receive impressions from the ocean and the special areas in this place. If you have a question, ask it. The ocean has many wonderful things to share with you, so bathe in it often for renewal of body and mind. Bathe in it now and watch what arises in your feelings and imagination.

9 If you look behind you, you will see four more doors: two on each side of the blue door. To the far left is the door to your existence through all time; it holds all that your being has experienced through eternity. The door on the immediate left of the blue door is an entrance into the inner life of other people; through it you can gain insight into those you love, in order to help and counsel them. The door on the right of the blue door leads to healing of yourself or others. The door on the far right leads to the universal wisdom that Life holds. Enter with care and respect any of the doors that you choose to explore.

Connections beyond yourself

Have other human beings in the past created a frontier post in the dimension of sleep and death? Do they now live there, just as you live in the physical world? Can you learn to wake up in that world and develop not simply a few minutes of excitement, but a dwelling place, a place of work, of relationships and exploration within the dimension of bodyless and deathless experience?

This is such a magnificent possibility, such an unprecedented step forward in human evolution, that it is difficult to grasp why the history books don't focus on the first human beings to achieve full and lasting awareness in sleep. Why don't they honour these men and women as the magnificent trail-blazers of a path that has opened us to transcendence of personal or planetary death? This is also the doorway to the stars, and makes our tin cans of spacecraft look ridiculous.

GIANTS OF THE BODYLESS STATE

For many hundreds of years in the Far East a culture developed that had as its vital centre the exploration of consciousness. Human beings rose from their birth in jungle surroundings to become giants in their ability to live beyond the frontier of sleep and death. Life and death became, for them, a single territory. Even before their bodies aged and died, they had entered the bodyless state and knew it as home. Some of those early explorers became permanently lucid. While sitting quietly, they demonstrated constant awareness of what people were doing at great distances.

When you enter lucidity, you cannot help at some point meeting one or more of these giants. If you are lucky or worthy, you will find yourself being taught or sustained by such a being. Even masters of lucidity in recent times, such as Aurobindo

Ghose, the Indian philosopher, poet and mystic, have worked with people while they slept and dreamed.

As you become more lucid in your dreams and in waking, you will gradually be aware of the connections that you have, at this level, with those you love, and with those to whom you are linked by affinities, interests and common goals (such as the spiritual work you undertake). Sometimes this arises as a deeply felt understanding of particular past cultures, and of their way of life and the wisdom at which they arrived. Sometimes the connections you develop lead you to do specific work in your waking life. Finding love at that level is also extraordinary. You may meet someone in your dream life who lives half a world away from you and yet has deep links of understanding and love with you. Then gradually you find each other in waking life. That is a very special thing.

The most enduring aspect of such connections is that your life develops meaning and dimensions it never previously had. You sense great depths within yourself; you feel more whole as a person. You know that you have a meaningful place in the world, and are more capable of living and loving in it.

Linking with others

One dream researcher with great initiative and wide vision discovered that individuals in the dream groups he ran were having insightful (and sometimes healing) dreams about each other. He went on to encourage people to dream in this way, recognizing that while dreaming you can reach into the lives of others.

The more lucid you are in your dreams or in waking, the more this becomes possible. The many reasons you wish to meet one of your family, a friend, a loved one or a stranger can also operate at the lucid level. You may desire to understand what is really going on in a child; what could resolve a friend's problem; how to

develop a loving relationship at a distance; or even to check someone's state of health. Of course, the simple wish to communicate in a fuller way than words or distance permit may be your prime motivation.

MEET WITH OTHERS

You can arrange to meet on certain nights with other people who are interested in lucidity. This enables you to increase your own lucidity, because when one of the group becomes lucid, he or she can 'wake' others in the group. It also enables you to test your lucidity by checking what happens within the group. One dream experienced by a member of such a group was as follows:

There were six or more people sleeping on mattresses on the floor. Two or three of them were awake, sitting up. They had small pointed hats, such as Tibetan Lamas have. I realized this meant they had reached a point of growth where they could wake up in dreams. We talked together and then were going to start waking the others.

DEEPENING AND CLARIFYING

You can decide to meet someone to deepen or clarify your relationship with them. It is worth making such meetings a regular event, as this helps to develop and train your lucid dreaming.

CREATING A MEETING PLACE

You can create a meeting place where those you are involved with can gather. Remember that whatever you think and feel becomes an external reality at this level. You can visualize the setting or building in which you want to meet. Create it either as an individual or as a group, by carefully visualizing all the details of it. Neuropsychiatrist Dr Karagulla (see pages 75 and 91), in interviewing lucid dreamers, found that some of them often attended places of learning while they slept, and recalled detailed information about what was learned. In some cases two people attending the same place of learning could remember exactly the same information.

Lucidity gives you entrance to a new territory. From what has been learned – not yet by science, but certainly by

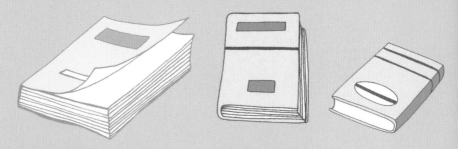

individual explorers – this is just as valid a territory to live in as the Earth. We do not know how many individuals and intelligences beyond our understanding exist and have their home in that dimension. No doubt it is like our external universe: vast beyond comprehension. One social psychologist described his experience of it by saying that, while lucid, he went deeply into the possibilities of the dream process. By doing this he came to an environment that expressed itself as images of a resort where beings other than humans existed. Some of these beings were so different to anything he knew that he couldn't understand them in his lucid dream state.

One of the greatest aspects of lucidity is allowing you entrance into waking life of a new and transforming power that changes you individually, and through you, your loved ones and all the people around you.

MERGING WITH OTHERS

In the section on out-of-body-experiences (see pages 58–61), Rachel travelled from Germany to her home in London. At one point, although her mother was not consciously aware of Rachel's presence, a part of her knew and was united with her. In the dimension of lucidity, your body is simply a form that you adopt because it is familiar to you. It is a way of maintaining a sense of your identity amidst the enormous range of possibilities, but you do not have the fixed boundaries of your skin or your fingertips.

Because of that, Rachel was at one with her mother's mind, and knew her in a way that is usually impossible. This is one of the great features of extending your awareness into lucidity. You can (as one

THE INNER VISION

With a partner who is ready to explore lucid dreaming with you, you can make an agreement to meet and look at each other in more than a superficial way. Agree that you will merge together to a point that is mutually acceptable, to see what you can learn about, and from, each other.

1 Give each other a personal object, small enough to be held in the hand.

2 As you go to sleep, say to yourself aloud that you are going to become lucid and meet your partner. The object that you are holding (and continue to hold as you go to sleep) will help you become lucid.

3 When you meet, reach out to each other with a welcome feeling and open yourself to your partner. At that point, imagine that you are entering into their being – like stepping inside them. As you do this, observe whatever change of feelings you experience.

4 When you wake, even if you cannot remember a lucid dream, lie quietly and observe what you feel and what thoughts come to you. They are often highly relevant.

science-fiction writer put it) swap minds. You can merge into one another as much, or as little, as is mutually agreed. You learn and grow and become much richer in life experience and knowledge. This is not so strange as you do it all the time when you learn from other people or when you love another person; at those times you absorb huge amounts of information from them. During lucidity this can happen faster and more fully than while awake.

Dreaming with a partner

Exploring the world of dreams with a partner is one of the most intimate relationships you can have. Although a great deal of learning and growth is possible in such a relationship, it is not always easy. In the lucid and dreaming condition it is more difficult to hide who you are. Whatever you undertake with a partner will have added power, because of the fundamental law that in this dimension the desires of a single person have less effect than those of two or more people. Here are a few suggestions that you can explore together.

CREATE A DREAM HOUSE OR SANCTUARY

A few years ago my best friend Kevin died. Shortly afterwards I had a lucid dream in which we were walking together and talking. Kevin was complaining that he couldn't find a home. He had a rough beginning in life, having been in an orphanage, and feeling 'homeless' was a lifelong problem. So, putting my arm around his shoulder, I said to him, 'Kevin, you are dead! If you think like this here, you will create a hell for yourself. So let's

build you a home.' Kevin began to get the idea, and the scenery gradually changed. He created a sunny walled courtyard, with vines and other plants, with an adjoining house. The rock-built house had a room with a huge window with a view overlooking the sea.

Things can be built and changed fast in the dimension of dreams. So, with your partner, carefully plan what you want. Talk over and define the details. If possible, draw it to create a clear image in your mind. Then take it into a mutual visualization. The world of lucidity is a very real place, so don't think of what you are doing as a meaningless fantasy. You are building something that has an existence just as real as any concept or idea – and remember: ideas can influence millions of people. Follow through by deciding to have a lucid dream in which you enter your new home or sanctuary.

LOOK FOR YOUR 'AKASHIC RECORDS'

Akasha is a word defining something that early travellers in the lucid dimension discovered. It refers to the fundamental substance of the universe. The early

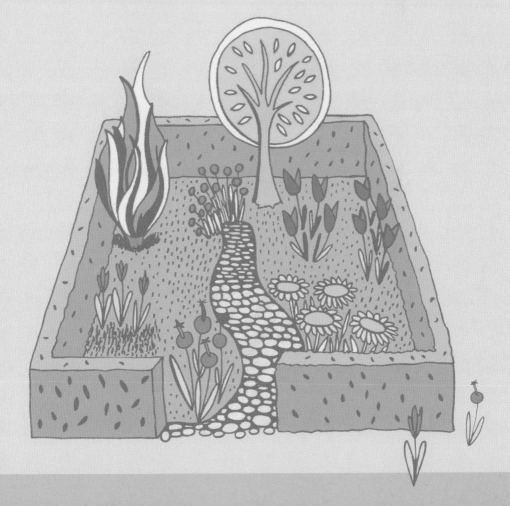

explorers found that every shift in the unfolding universe left a record on the Akasha – these are known as the Akashic records, and include a history of every individual. But, as each individual has two aspects (an eternal undying, and a transient self that lives and dies), the Akashic records hold the memory of all the many personalities that your eternal being has projected into time and space. So if you are a loving couple, the records will tell when you have been together in the past.

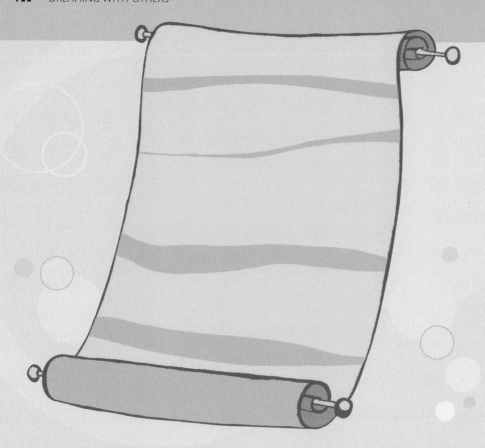

In seeking your Akashic records, recognize that this is not simply a game. Remembrance brings change and responsibility.

Imagine, as you plan your lucid time together, that you are looking backwards along a beam of light that has projected your present life. Feel the sense of travelling back along that beam to its source, and looking at the traces or memories from which your present life has arisen. Unless you are adept in lucidity, this will not come at your first attempt. But keep moving through the obstacles that arise until you get a comprehensible insight. When you arrive, you will know, because your insight will enable you to make real life changes, unfold new skills and know innate weaknesses.

EXPERIENCE THE WONDER OF SEX IN MUTUAL MERGING

Some references to sex in lucidity involve doing things like putting butterscotch on the sexual organs and licking it off. However, if that is what you want to do, it can surely be done while you are awake.

Such action misses the glorious possibilities of love and sex during lucidity. At that level, love is a splendour that irradiates the whole of life. Sex merges you and the person you love together at all levels. It's a giving and receiving from which you can emerge a new person. It's a return to a primal level of yourself and of creation.

Yes, in dreams you do have (or can have) a very full and varied sexual experience. But I believe that in our depths we are seeking something more than genital sex. We seek union, completeness, a companion who is in some way a complementary aspect of us. We seek the joy that flows through us in magnificent sharing of who we are.

If you have a partner with whom you wish to explore the many dimensions of love, talk to each other openly about dreaming together and discovering further depths of togetherness. Plan how and where you are going to meet and love. Make a contract and, before sleeping, go through whatever ritual of washing or preparation you would use in waking. Then determine to meet each other lucidly.

ENTER THE ENERGY FLUX

In the dimension of dreams there is the possibility of many people merging to form a new condition. You can see something of this when groups of people unite their efforts, influence and money to achieve something. In lucidity, it can become a merging of personal strengths and abilities in a healing, balancing way. In it you merge with others, without losing your identity. Entering the flux brings a living connection with purposes beyond your own life, and opens you to energies that are flowing into human existence from the cosmic mind. New ways of being human are emerging.

To enter the flux, first imagine it as a wall of energy – perhaps like countless cells, but without physical substance. Realize that it is made of many beings who have merged. Then slowly walk into the energy and open yourself to the healing and wholeness that enters into you. If you are lucid in your dream, ask to be led to the flux. A simple request is enough to produce a response. Entering the flux unites the many facets of yourself.

Being a healing channel

Within lucidity there are countless ways of working with other people to heal and help. The lucid dream in which I helped my friend Kevin build a home (see page 120) showed a healing action. You can bring about healing change because you are awake to things that the person whom you are helping is not aware of. In Kevin's case, he was not recognizing that he was dead and there were completely different possibilities open to him than when he was alive.

So working with those who have died is one possibility. Everyone at some time faces the death of a friend or relative, but if you have worked with the principles given in this book, you have a guide to helping when that happens. The help to offer is usually that of recognizing that the person in question is dead, and what the possibilities are within their new existence. Beyond that, there is the need for them to gradually digest and integrate their life experience. As you extend your ability to be lucid in dreaming and waking, you will be in a position not only to help, but also to learn as you relate to the dead. They too pass through stages of growth.

BE A HEALING CHANNEL

Try this simple form of healing.

1   Use the exercise on opening to your core (see page 67).

2   Keeping that as a background feeling, link it to a person (or people) to whom you wish to let life and love flow, by creating a mental image of this.

3   If the person in question has a specific problem, hold an image of the flow from your core washing that away. There is no need to struggle with this; let it happen effortlessly.

4   Hold this image for a few minutes and then let it go.

One of the great methods of healing is akin to dreamwork. In other words, you work with the virtual-reality or dream world in which the person you are helping is located. As you learn to stabilize your lucidity, you can move about in the other person's dream and help them: either waking them up to see what is happening or shifting their dream environment. The following dream that Teresa had illustrates this:

I and others were helping a man who insisted on living in a small stable-like room that was foul with his faeces and urine. He wouldn't go out or clean it, and his clothes were filthy too. He wouldn't be helped, and blamed his condition on anything – and anyone – but himself. However, we managed to help him accept responsibility for his condition. He came out of the stable and then happily asked if we could put his clothes in a washing machine. This enabled him to start a new life.

The dirt this man was living within was his own negative emotions and attitudes, which kept him trapped in a very limited life. And although the change brought about was at the level of his unconscious, it did emerge into his waking life.

HEALING YOURSELF

Because you create your own world in dreams, many of the situations that you meet will be reflections of your own condition that needs to be dealt with. Here is Carl's description of encountering such a personal situation:

The only way I can describe what happened is to say that I was lucid and wandering around a big, dark building. I realized this meant that I was exploring the dungeons of myself. I didn't know where I was going, but I was led into a dark cellar, and there, curled up, was a little boy. I was deeply

shocked, because I realized this child had been locked in there alone for years. I tried to get near, but he shouted to me, 'I don't want anybody near me. I'm dangerous. Keep away.'

Being awake to what was happening, I realized this was myself, hurt as a young boy and trapped in the misery I then felt. I knew too that his being 'dangerous' was a defence against being hurt again. So I said to him, 'How old are you, little dangerous being?' He said, 'I'm three. I'm only little. But I'm dangerous. I will KILL YOU *if you get near me. I'll bite you or something.'*

There followed a two-way communication too long to report. But Carl gradually gained the child's trust, and the boy was taken into the man's arms. In this way he recovered a precious part of himself and became more whole. This sort of healing (with oneself or someone else) concerns the gradual development of a trusting relationship, through which real change can be effected. But sometimes it also means meeting emotional pain, which needs to be released before change can come about.

HEALING OTHERS

One of the classic forms of healing is opening to the power at your core and directing it into another person's life. Although everyone has the ability to do this, some people have enormous skill in it. The exercise in which you opened to your core (see page 67) laid the foundation for this type of healing. In using this approach, it is easy to slip into the mistaken attitude that you have to be somebody very special to do this, or that you have to concentrate like mad to make it happen. This is not so.

In fact, the opposite it true. Your core exists already; it is self-existent. You do not need to develop it, or earn it, by being 'spiritual' or good. It is already yours. However, you may not be able to surrender yourself enough to let it flow out of you. Your determined attempts to heal others may be getting in the way of the flow. The more you relax, the more that ever-shining radiance will flow out of you. You have to recognize that you are not the healer. Your visualization of healing flowing to another person is a circuit or channel through which the energy of life flows.

Group energy

Considering how lonely many people feel, and how depressed or isolated they are, it seems a part of the human condition to feel separated from each other by real distances. We see ourselves as physically isolated. This is a strange illusion, considering that everything around us connects us with other people in a real, physical way.

For instance, it is probably true to say that you didn't make your own clothes; you didn't grow your own food; and you didn't generate the electricity coming into your home. You do not drill your own teeth, or operate on your own appendix if it is diseased. You depend upon teachers for your children, and on millions of other people for transport, building homes, making you laugh or singing to you. You are completely immersed in other people. It is only by cooperative effort that most of the things around you exist. Life itself – the working together of cells, and the interplay of different organs and systems in your body – is an extraordinary example of cooperative action. What you probably fail to realize is that you, as an individual, are just as much a cell in a great organism as the cells in your body are.

Although you can see the result of cooperation or group action, it is sometimes difficult to grasp its essence. It always stays hidden as it flows through the cosmos, creating the enormity of galaxies beyond measure. But it *is* active in your life all the time, and if you can begin to recognize group action, then you can work with it – and everything that happens to you is part of that action.

GOING WITH THE FLOW

One dreamer, Sarah, lucidly entered a dream and found herself seeing her life rocked by waves of influence, which passed through her and moved her – like being part of a flock of flying birds. That was a glorious feeling. It felt like a huge and wonderful anthem of life in which she was involved, and she saw herself as part of an immense process. Sarah also felt that she needed to let herself move with these enormous currents.

Tuning in to the vast, but subtle, currents that flow around you is like swimming in the direction of the current in a river. You move faster. You not only have your own power, but that of the current, too. In life, this means that you can achieve more and find greater satisfaction. In the world of lucidity enormous changes are emerging. You may feel these as subtle energies, which gradually take on form and become real in the world.

LONG-TERM CHANGE

There are things you can do to find your place in these flows of creative energy. What follows isn't a specific exercise in the way the previous exercises were. Rather, it suggests long-term directions you can take in life.

Buried deep within you is the seed of something you want to do, be or become during your life. It is a seed that ultimately wants to bear fruit, before death ends this cycle of your experience. That seed differs with each person. However, what is common to all is that what grows within you, and moves towards bearing fruit, does so only in relationship with others and with the subtle processes of Life. So the question to ask yourself is: What is your life plan, individually and in the scheme of things? Use the approaches you have already practised to pursue the question. Take it into a lucid dream by visualizing yourself waking and asking the question. Then, watch what changes occur around you, and what you gain insight into. If you don't reach lucidity, record your dreams and explore what they depict; it can help to take to bed with you an object representing your question. Hold it as you sleep, and realize that it is there to call a meaningful dream from your dream maker.

COSMIC CHANGES

Many people read newspapers or trade journals to see what the latest events and trends are. But behind all this lie huge cosmic trends, filtering into human events. To gain a look at these trends, first imagine you are standing back from human evolution and getting an overview of it. There is a constant flow, from primitive creatures that didn't stand upright, through many evolutionary changes, to today's human experience. Then pose a question concerning what influences are playing upon human life now. What is emerging in individuals, and in the human race overall, that impinges upon your life? Pursue this question as described above.

SEARCH FOR LOVED ONES

Looking at life from the vantage point of lucidity, it can be seen that humans come into life to accomplish certain things. We have links with people – only some of whom we know. We are part of a group endeavour in some way. You may not yet have met a

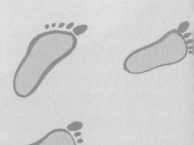

loving and cooperative partner in life. But in your lucidity you can reach out to find those people with whom you have a deep kinship, with whom you are working or whom you love, but have not yet made physical contact. This search takes time, but be persistent. At first it will be merely an intimation in your dreams. Then it will clarify and become real in your waking life. Approach this search in the way described above.

Life is an adventure in which you are not alone. Your links with others are many and varied. To uncover them brings depths of meaning to your present existence, so search the trails of your dreams for the footprints of those who walk with you.

Tapping the cosmic mind

It is possible that the universe is like a giant hologram. Every part of a hologram, if cut up, has a complete picture within it – and so it is with the universe. Any tiny fragment of it (such as a skin cell) connects with the whole. If you look deeply enough into yourself, you will find all history and all the cosmos. Cayce, the healer who was consulted by the White House (see page 75), daily displayed the ability to tap this wealth of information. And, from his excursions into the cosmic mind, he dictated 14,000,000 words while asleep.

Many people who have had a near-death experience report what they term a 'life review', during which they live again every moment, every thought and every fleeting impression of their life, and experience the impact of their words or deeds on those around them. Such accounts have been reported in every age and every culture – all of them remarkably similar – and show an extraordinary human ability to know more, gain much deeper insights and digest experience. Unfortunately, we have been taught to see ourselves as isolated from the wider world around us.

LEARNING TO LISTEN

One specialist in neurophysiology says that when the mathematics of quantum-level particles and the human brain are compared, they are the same. In other words, human brains and physiology are not isolated from their surroundings, but enfolded in the larger cosmic processes. In fact, the descriptions of spiritual experiences parallel the descriptions of quantum physics. That is why the physicist Fritjof Capra wrote the book *The Tao of Physics* (Flamingo, 1992). What I want to get across is that drawing from the cosmic mind is not something accessible

only to yogis or mystics. It is an everyday part of your experience – if you can just learn to listen.

If you have been using the exercises and techniques in this book, you have probably noticed an increase in your intuitive awareness of what is happening around you. This is the first stage in experiencing a greater involvement with Life. Earlier I called this 'cosmic consciousness' and pointed out that it is possibly an emerging stage of evolution.

The universe is an ocean of sentience. You are already swimming in that ocean, and you are conscious because the universe knows itself through you. It knows itself as you. That you are barely aware of who you are proves nothing. That you can gradually become more aware of your existence as a fundamental part of the universe is the essence of this book.

PROBE FURTHER

Previous exercises have given you the first steps in tapping the resources of the cosmos. What comes next is to get a feel (not just an idea) for what it means to approach the ocean of Life.

1 Create a feeling or sense, not just of the world around you, not just of the whole globe of the Earth, not just of this galaxy – but of the innumerable galaxies. Sense them as your extended being.

2 Perhaps this is beyond imagining, but try to get a feel for it. Take in these two points: how are you going to open yourself to this sublime mystery that is the universe, of which you are a part? And how have you treated the universe? The universe is everything around you. It says to you, 'Whatever you have done to the smallest of creatures around you, you have done to *me*.' Entering the wider life is all about relationships.

3 When you take in those two points and feel them, you have the beginning of finding the More that you are. Then you are open.

TOUCHING THE SUBLIME

During my thirties, when I was struggling to understand exactly how the cosmic mind enters into our experience, something extraordinary happened. I had got up in the middle of the night to go to the toilet. Sleepily I started to climb back into bed when a voice, everywhere in the room, said, 'You have asked how God touches your life – now watch closely.'

Ever since then I have watched closely how the sublime touches people's lives. In doing so I have learned the following interesting points.

The sublime can express itself in two main ways: either as an inner experience or insight, or as an outer event. But the ways in which this is done are incredibly varied. The mechanism involved when the sublime is experienced inwardly usually involves dreams. My experience of the voice, for instance, was the dream process – full-surround virtual reality – in action while I was awake.

Any of the senses or different ways of experiencing can be used. This includes seeing colours, people or animals, smelling scents, hearing a voice or some music, and body sensations.

When the communication comes from outside, it might be through a strange coincidence, an event that is obviously a response to a question you have asked, or something you have been looking for.

A SENSE OF BELONGING

One of the deepest human drives – one that has lasted throughout human evolution from the earliest of times – is to feel a sense of belonging or being of value in the scheme of things. This drive, and many of the enlightening insights that men and women have garnered from their personal relationship with the cosmos, have been enshrined in different world religions. In her book *Collision with the Infinite* (Windrush Press, 1996), Suzanne Segal calls this 'the vastness'. Your own personal meeting with it will also have a sense of the holy. It doesn't take away all ills, but it does offer you a surety that you are part of an eternal life. It will leave you transformed.

The great adventure

Your life is the grand adventure. You are the heroine or hero of the drama. The challenge is to be as much as you can be in the circumstances that you face, and with as much love as possible. Lucidity is one of the magic charms you have to help you find your way through the maze. Along the way you have a mission to fulfil. There is no set task that everyone has in common. Each of us has something different to do. So part of the challenge is to discover what your own mission is and then set about it.

Explorers of lucidity have, collectively, revealed what they understand of the principles underlying life's adventure. Free will is a fundamental part of it. Of course, a perfect world could exist completely controlled by a 'good God'. But that would mean that we were all robots. With free will, the core of your being enters into an experience of physical life again and again, gradually learning to manifest its innate potential in the difficult three-dimensional world of the body.

Although humans are physically small, fragile creatures, the

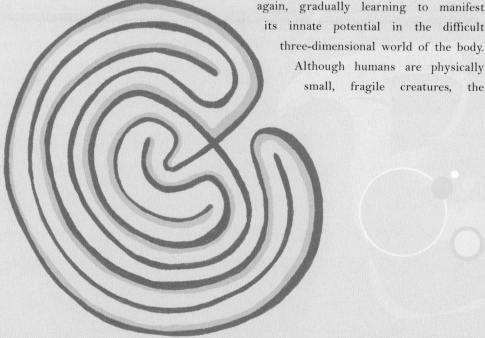

potential of the human spirit can be seen in the incredible range of the human mind and imagination.

DUAL ASPECTS

The core self is both male and female, but assumes a gender in the body. And the personality that forms is usually only a facet of the core self, and it begins to realize the distinction between these two aspects only as it grows in awareness. If great progress is made in life, the personality displays multiple talents as it draws more and more into expression in the body.

At times the waking personality gains an insight into its core self, and produces life changes that are inexplicable when seen from the viewpoint of the body being the only reality. In one near-death case, a woman was shown a photograph of researcher Dr Raymond Moody while she was apparently physically dead, and was told his name. This happened in 1971, before she knew anything about him or his work, and well before Moody published his book *Life After Life* (Bantam, 1983) about near-death experiences. Four years later Moody moved to the same street where the woman lived. During Hallowe'en, Moody's son knocked on the woman's door trick-or-treating. When she heard his surname, she asked him to tell his father that she needed to talk to him. Moody then visited the woman and heard her extraordinary story first hand.

All of us have these two lives. One life takes place within often enormous limitations, as a personality experiencing physical life. The other is as a huge and timeless being, who has dipped into time and physical life again and again; this being has links of love and work beyond what we usually know. Only as we become more lucid in waking and sleeping do we begin to realize the enormity of who we are. This is the spiritual path taken by men and women down the ages. This is the path we take going home.

Who can you be today?

When you achieve greater lucidity, you discover you are not alone on this planet. There are beings you meet who have trodden this path long before you, or who are way ahead of you and no longer need to live a physical life. Some of these beings are so incredible they are beyond what we can understand. To touch such wonders of what astrophysicist Jacques Valle calls the 'Multiverse' – the multiple dimensions of the universe – is to have a wider and nobler vision of life. It is to live within something with vaster possibilities than are offered by our usual view of the universe and our place on this planet.

OPENING YOURSELF TO WONDER

So today, this moment, here and now, you can open to being more than you have ever been before. Recognize how limiting beliefs create actual walls that hem you in. Realize that at this moment, if you drop away the views and beliefs you were probably taught since childhood, you open yourself to a wider and more wondrous life. Now, at this moment, you can swim in that ocean of life and love that constantly gives you existence. No thunderclap needs to sound for this to happen. No lightning bolt needs to strike you. It is here, now, within the ordinary sounds and events surrounding you. Here it is, interwoven with all that you think and feel. Why not open yourself to this experience and let yourself know it?

HARNESS YOUR IMAGINATION

Today, here and now, recognize that your thoughts and imagination are not useless fantasy. They are the subtlest of threads, out of which you weave the substance of your life and love. They are the tenderest shoots of what can grow into a massive tree of life. Out of them you create wonderful possibilities or machines of destruction; you open doors or build castle walls; you create your life. When Walt

Disney fantasized his characters, he was not living a useless daydream. His acceptance of his imagination was the subtle reality upon which he built a whole industry. So now, today, be aware of your power of creation. Recognize it and look to see what world it is that you are making. Take care, and work with love and with the best in you to form what in the end is all you have – your life.

Today, this moment, remember that you are capable of creating the full-surround virtual reality that we call a dream. Remember too that every night you create a new drama. You conjure out of yourself the people, creatures and surroundings of your dream. Then you give life to what you create – not only life, but purpose and drama. You are a supreme dramatist, playwright, actor and actress. You are the great Creator – in your dreams. Considering this, have you ever wondered why that enormous creativity does not flow into your waking life? You can see that some people have that creativity and are enriched by it personally and financially. Let it happen to you!

Today, now, remember a few well-known facts about how you encounter the so-called 'real' world of waking life. First, when you look at an object such as an orange or apple, remember that although you have the sense of seeing what colour and texture the fruit has, in fact all you are seeing is reflected light. You never see the actual colour of the object. Your eyes take in streams of light that are translated into nervous impulses, which are transmitted along the optic nerve. In the brain those nerve impulses are again translated into an image that enables you to have some relationship with an apparently external world. In the same way, the nerve endings on your fingers transmit signals that are translated into sensation. In no way do you have a direct awareness of what you are 'looking' at. In no way do you really know what is around you. As in a dream, you are creating a full-surround virtual reality.

SWIMMING IN THE WATERS OF LIFE

Perhaps, if you could really see and know what you are, it would be a wave in an ocean of energy – only with a sense of your independence in your particular wave formation or movement. The wave is, out of its movement and form, a separate being. Yet at the same time it is inseparable from the ocean that gives it existence. Today, now, remember that you are in that

ocean. Sometimes take off the clothing you wear – created out of the images you have conceived of who you are and how you exist – and dive naked into that sea. Swim in it, play and be part of your natural infinite surroundings.

When you are in the ocean that is your real home, look around for the others who swim with you. Feel the great currents that carry you along, and ask yourself where they are going and where they came from.

Look back on what you perhaps viewed to be your 'real' life and see it from this new perspective. See it overall, and see the seeds from which it grew and the fruit it seeks to bear. And when you see that, ask for wisdom and strength to enable you to bring those fruits to ripeness.

Look for me there, for there is much more to share with you than can be expressed within this small book. There I swim with you and am known as Dreamhawk. If our paths have meaning together, I will take you to meet some of those great beings, who are to us like mountains that we stand before in awe. There we will bathe in the waters of life together and be renewed.

Index

Acknowledgements

Executive Editor Brenda Rosen
Editor Charlotte Wilson
Executive Art Editor Sally Bond
Designer Annika Skoog for Cobalt Id
Illustrator Sandra Howgate
Production Manager Louise Hall